Developing Effective Managers

Developing Effective Managers

A New Approach to
Business Education

REGINALD W. REVANS

LONGMAN

LONGMAN GROUP LIMITED
London

*Associated companies, branches and representatives
throughout the world*

© 1971 Praeger Publishers, Inc.

First published in this edition 1971
ISBN 0 582 44547 7
Published in the United States of America in 1971
by Praeger Publishers, Inc.
Printed in Great Britain by William Clowes and Sons Limited, London
Beccles and Colchester

To Hans Hellwig

Contents

Foreword

It has been a common and continuous charge against many, if not most, programs of management education that, in them, theory and practice have rarely supported each other. Few schools make explicit the theory of learning by experienced adults on which their syllabuses are presumably based. Still fewer design their courses around any general theory of managerial action—certainly not upon any theory of action reflecting the manager's world in field studies of such comprehensive rigor as would be demanded of a respectable theory in, say, biology. And what papers describing original research do appear in management literature are not usually about the real time activities of management as such: They are generally about economics, or mathematics, or psychology, or other established disciplines. And even if they are then of some relevance to industry or commerce, it is not always easy to see this relevance in terms of management action or management education.

It was to bridge the gap between theory and practice, between university and enterprise, between professor and manager, that the *Fondation Industrie-Université* was established in 1956. At that time, a group of industrialists who were aware of the problem sought to establish an institution to help them in improving the management of their firms. Rather than set up one large school for the whole of Belgium, they chose a more difficult solution: the creation of a nucleus at the heart of each university for encouraging management ideas, all coordinated by the *Fondation*. This system of decentralization has proved its effectiveness: On account of it, management studies in Belgium have become the joint concern of all the universities and of the whole of industry. Our teachers have developed in these centers, and bring to their work, a sense of the realities of business life; the industrialists are not longer reluctant to seek the help of the faculty on their operational problems. There now exists in Belgium a true spirit of mutual understanding, or reciprocal profit, that owes much to the *Fondation*.

It was therefore natural that Reginald W. Revans, as a former president of the European Association of Management Training Centers, should become interested in our work; it was also natural that, on reading in the British press that a large business school offering management courses of a conventional type was to be established at his own university, he should leave to join us in Brussels. He first worked to encourage the development of studies in managerial action; later, with the support of the *Fondation* and of our five Belgian university management centers, he turned his attention to integrating such action into the very development of the managers themselves. What has been achieved is described in this book; perhaps it will now be possible to move still further toward the integration of theory and practice in the management field. For example, all the universities of Belgium plan to offer a doctoral program in management science in which clinical skill will be demanded no less than intellectual talent. The university representatives have resolved to exalt the practical tasks of taking action in real time as well as the theoretical exercises of talking about taking action *sub specie aeternitatis*. The ideas set forth in this book may suggest a useful point of entry to this perilous mission.

Another obvious zone for fresh discovery—and one of great interest to the *Fondation*—is the learning process, not only of the experienced individual but also of the social organism that is the enterprise. Conventional courses may well be kept going by the belief (largely untested) that they improve the individuals who take them, but it is the change and growth process in the group, in the industrial community, in the company, and in our wider society that grants us final success. We are still far from understanding what this process of collective change and growth may be, much less from knowing how individual managers may initiate and control it.

Since genuine progress is achieved, in this imperfect world, only when reasonable men disagree—and are also able to agree on the boundaries of their disagreement—and since this book suggests what progress is possible in the unification of theory and practice, it follows that some of what Revans has to say will be taken by his academic colleagues as provocative: indeed, sometimes as downright ill-mannered. But, when important issues are involved, it is as well to illuminate both sides of them; and if—as implied here—the academic sponsorship of management education may sometimes concentrate too closely on what are claimed to be intellectual arguments, often *a priori* and abstract, it may be necessary for us to resort to an exchange upon the battlefield of the emotions. Certainly there are goals in developing managers that will never be reached by purely intellectual debate, much less by purely didactic exercises: Specialized or expert teachers, for example, inadequate to the task of examining the totality of management practice, will rarely be convinced of their inadequacy by merely consulting the contents of their intelligence. It might be easier to say to them in so many words that they are actually wasting the time of their students and thus bring their indignation to the rescue.

This book is not sparing of such inelegance: It suggests that, on some issues, the whole movement in management education is misconceived. So sweeping a thesis is not likely to be seen in other than emotional terms. Nevertheless, whether it is the author who is out of step or his critics remains to be seen. I personally feel that some of what he has to say could be debated with profit in other fields of professional education as well, and we should welcome the challenge he has thrown us. Innovation, in thought and action alike, must come to management education sooner or later. What is clear is that this book will have its impact, emotional no less than intellectual.

GASTON DEURINCK
Managing Director, Fondation Industrie-Université, Brussels

September, 1970

Preface

On February 1, 1969, a party of twenty-one Belgian managers arrived in America; they had come to discuss, with professors at leading business schools and consultants from some of the world's largest corporations, a range of strategic problems encountered by their firms. To this extent, nothing was novel about their visit. In one way, however, it was probably unusual: each fellow had come to talk about the problem posed not by his own firm but by another also represented in the party.

For several months, each of the visitors had worked full time in an enterprise other than his own, attacking a major managerial problem which he had not attacked before; in his pocket, he carried both a report of how he now saw the problem and a draft plan for dealing with it after he had returned to Europe. One fellow, normally an adviser to a world oil corporation on issues of planning and logistics, had come to report on his progress in helping one of Belgium's leading banks to clarify its changing relations with the economy as a whole. Another, responsible for technological research in a nonferrous-metals company, was helping a large steel firm to determine the conditions necessary for success in product innovation. A third, recently nominated to take charge of an economic planning unit within his own steel concern, was spending his year designing strategies for the development of a long-established paper firm. Here, at last, was a community whose members actually lived by doing each other's jobs, by promoting an exchange of tasks and responsibilities on which they had already spent five months' full time.

Three weeks later, they were back in their Belgian foster enterprises, where they remained until the end of June, 1969, guiding whatever resources they themselves could generate or could deflect from other channels into a first solution of the policy problems that had been their principal interest since the previous summer. Thus, their labors did not remain entirely diagnostic; half their time was devoted to getting something done about their findings. This involvement in action elsewhere was the central, and perhaps distinctive, theme of the program.

Accompanying the party were members of the staff of each of the five Belgian university management centers, which, with the firms, made up this pioneering consortium. The twenty-one fellows were, throughout the program, distributed in small groups among these management centers, and for three reasons: to give to, and receive from, a few others the support that membership of a small group permits; to keep side by side those whose projects seemed to attack related problems; and to bring the research and teaching staff of the university business centers, both to advise and to learn, closely into association with what the fellows were trying to do.

There were, thus, three operational parties to the experiment: those learning to attack strategic problems simply by attacking them, the enterprises offering the problems to be attacked, and the universities suggesting some of the analytical weapons to be used and the operational tactics to be deployed. But there was a fourth party, the accoucheur of the whole undertaking, who had first made possible this novel exchange of managerial confidence and, even more remarkable, had contrived this cooperation among independent professors in remote universities. Such was the integrating genius provided by *La Fondation*

Industrie-Université, set up more than a decade earlier as an administrative device to ensure that the contacts between Belgium's industry and commerce, on the one hand, and its university teachers of management, on the other, were realistic, productive, and economical. Without the past achievements and present reputation of the *Fondation*, the consortium could never have been imagined, let alone set up and made to work successfully. Belgium may well have the administrative advantages of a small nation, but the real secret of its success in launching this program was the early victory of the *Fondation* over the isolating specialism and normative abstraction that are too often the final travesties of academic freedom. For thirteen years, Belgium's five independent management schools had been learning to work together by contributing to joint training courses, joint research programs, and the preparation of joint reports on educational policy. Nor is this all. The program, like all cooperative excursions, already shows by its promises of success, and equally by its experiences of failure, what further essays in federation remain to be tried in the future. In a sense, the perpetual riddle to which the *Fondation* has for the past decade addressed its indefatigable spirit — How do scholarship and industry help each other? — is also the specific conundrum, writ large, at the heart of the report carried to America by every fellow — How can new ideas encourage this enterprise, and how can this enterprise encourage new ideas? The Inter-University Program for Advanced Management is also addressed to these questions of innovative symbiosis.

When the tripartite design of the program was first proposed, it was argued that the speed of events now makes it not only interesting to experiment with new methods of management education but imperative. By whatever industrial or commercial index one may measure, such as the fecundity of scientific research, the intensity of technological development, or the speed of data processing, it can be shown that there is now more change in the lifetime of one man than in the whole of previously recorded history. When events move fast, adjustment must move even faster. If the rate of change in the chemical industry is now a thousand times what it was a century ago, we may assert with confidence that the chemical industry faces problems of adjustment unknown to its ancestors. Whole organizations, not only selected individuals within them, must learn to adjust. There must be collective as well as occasional learning, institutional and social as well as personal and individual development. Moreover, because change has become the most significant feature of our economy, the managerial processes of absorbing it deserve no less to be understood than the technical advances of the particular industry being changed. We must prosecute research into the nature and conditions of strategic change just as conscientiously as we prosecute research into science and technology. Thus, the very speed of innovation and the setting of demands for a still speedier adjustment to it inescapably force the organization itself and the university research worker to enroll, as students of the general transformation process, alongside the manager within the program.

No doubt, this book is published at the wrong time, like every book that attempts to reflect a continuously evolving reality. In a formal sense, the program is now finished, and it may thus invite, and perhaps justify, description. The fellows are back at their own jobs, the members of the university staff are back in their lecture rooms, and the host enterprises are trying to exploit the gains in the battles so long contested. But the deeper effects are still unknown and must long so remain.

It might have been better, in the interests of scientific knowledge, to have reported on the experiment only after a fuller attempt had been made to assess and understand its ultimate consequences. Nevertheless, there is another point of view. Several professors with whom I have discussed the program insist that no announcement of our iconoclastic excursion could ever be premature. It is, in their view, never too soon to warn the worlds of business and learning against the perils of reality. Who can say what confronts the manager, abandoned to his own devices in the world of industry, unaided in observing what goes on, and unsupported in his struggles to improve it? Those who live by the academic tradition may share such solicitude. But the hybrid approach of this Belgian consortium, of theory-oriented professor and action-oriented manager, to the practical resolution of complex problems set away from each particular manager's normal pitch and from each professor's familiar rostrum seems to awaken a vivid curiosity in, and to have a compelling attraction for, all who have become engaged in it.

The book begins with a short description of the program as a whole, and then develops a model for relating practice to theory. A score of fellows have simultaneously attacked a score of strategic problems—similar in that all are unstructured and complex. They had, first, to agree on some common language in which to exchange their ongoing experiences for their own immediate operational use and, second, to write in their new language a code in which each problem may be both theoretically diagnosed and practically treated. As the projects developed, so did the search for a one-to-one correspondence between the common model and what the field managers did, or what the fellows would advise their supporting enterprises to do. In the jargon of statistics, it is possible to write the history of each of the twenty projects, as it unfolded, in a notation both amenable to factor analysis and intelligible to action-oriented decision-makers. The contents of this section will then represent the principal factors to be thrown out by the analysis. We have used three such ideas. They are here, from their symbiotic form, described as systems, all of which interact not only within themselves but with each other as well: system alpha, for defining what objectives the enterprises might choose to pursue; system beta, for suggesting the negotiations by which these objectives might be achieved; system gamma, for tracing the learning effects that this definition and this negotiation might have upon the managers, both fellows and collaborators, who undertook them. The validity of this section must depend upon not only whether it represents the common elements within the collective experience of the fellows (a descriptive model) but also whether it is likely to be useful to other managers as a guide to the formation of their strategic plans in the real world (a normative model).

That aspect of this general model mainly concerned with the learning processes of both fellows and managers is then taken up and expanded. Much of this may be speculative.

Nevertheless, I feel that any of us with ideas, however sketchy, on the learning processes of experienced adults should set them out for the benefit of others, if only as a warning against needless thought. The arts of management development seem to need all the support they can get from any learning theory,* however imperfect.

The most valuable part of the book comprises the reports of the fellows themselves on how they saw their experience, both in Belgium and in America, up to their return to their own firms. It may even be possible to continue with the consortium principle and to repeat the program, mainly on the basis of the proved and acceptable lessons of this pioneering effort, rather than on the untested assumptions with which the first attempt necessarily had to start. I should feel amply rewarded if the fellows recommended the Fondation to repeat the program in principle but to redesign it throughout in detail.

Finally, I may be allowed a brief apology. I am well aware that I do not share many of the present values of the academic world. My insistence that the first need of any science, namely, *that one should continuously observe its field of action at first hand* — that we should involve the managers themselves in collecting and interpreting the data necessary for successful decision-making — has been dismissed as unscientific, as poor research, and as unlikely to lead to any understanding of management, either as art or as science. I cannot reply to these arguments, simply because I do not understand them. I shall, however, cheerfully bear the reproach of conspiring to adulterate the standards of university scholarship. I conclude with a quotation from Hazlitt's essay "On the Ignorance of the Learned":

> Learning is, in too many cases . . . a substitute for true knowledge. Books are less often made use of as spectacles to look at nature with, than as blinds to keep out its strong light and

---

*A review of the poverty of our theories of learning and of creativity is to be found in the first few pages of Arthur Koestler's *The Ghost in the Machine*, published by Macmillan (New York) in 1967. He writes as though, after reading extensively in the field, he wishes still to know as little about psychological theories as do some of the psychologists who produce them.

shifting scenery from weak eyes and indolent dispositions . . .
The most sensible people to be met with in society are men of
business and of the world, who argue from what they see and
know, instead of spinning cobweb distinctions of what things
ought to be.

1

The Inter-University Program for
Advanced Management

THE NEED FOR INDIVIDUAL DEVELOPMENT

The Inter-University Program for Advanced Management, involving the five universities of Belgium and twenty-one of its largest firms, and lasting from March, 1968, to July, 1969, strove essentially to achieve for industrial and commercial managers that cohesion between theory and practice demanded of all persons who must take undivided responsibility for their professional actions. It recognized that the role of the manager is fundamentally different from that of his adviser or of his teacher, whose tutorial responsibilities cannot underwrite the manager's personal decisions.[1] Thus, although additional book-learning is often an operational asset, every manager has two further needs, singular to himself, largely inaccessible to others, and, perhaps for that reason, often poorly perceived by the architects of teaching programs.[2] These needs are, first, to know how he, as the individual he happens to be, judges the practical utility, as distinct from the theoretical elegance, of scholarly subjects such as economics; second, to know how he applies their generalities to the specific conditions of an individual firm striving to ameliorate some particular problem — namely, to a total situation previously unknown and never to recur.

3

The first of these needs is to know what predisposing mental schemata or library of perceptual subroutines he carries around in his head ready to call forward into action; the second is to identify the uniqueness of each such call, in which every parameter is different from what last it was and from what it will be next. Thus every manager must first answer such questions about accounting theory, for example, as "How, if at all, does my acquaintance with it color my general outlook as a manager? How do I listen to the advice of accountants—with too much respect, or with too little? Can I really understand a complex transaction better if it is described in detailed accounting terms? If we should encounter trouble, how far could I clarify it by combing through the accounts? How do I put a value on what is not already priced, for example, the reputation of my firm or the worthwhileness of my job?" The answer to these questions will differ critically from manager to manager.

Second, the manager needs to ask by what sequence of steps he takes his action, unique to each different occasion, after reviewing a complex of factors of which many would be unintelligible in accounting, or even in quantitative, terms alone. There is a proverb: "To teach French to Tommy, it is necessary to know not only French but also Tommy." The program invoked the further condition that the manager must know not only, say, general accounting theory and the specific problem on which he is to use it; he must also know the manner in which he himself handles his own knowledge of them both. He must perceive himself as a unique integrator, unlike all others, having his own degree of willingness to take risks, his own system of values, his own estimates both of the trustworthiness of what is said to him and of the inner clarity with which he sees the prospect of his own reward. He must know not only how he *should* act, but also how he *does* act. It is no more possible to run a living business on an impersonal knowledge of management theory and of such objective data as accounts and sales records alone than it is to run a hospital only with physiologists, biochemists, radiographers, and other specialists, all with their different expertise, their particular scientific specimens, and their caballistic quantitative charts. The manager, like the clinician, must provide *his own personal integration* of the diversified resources of his field. Objective data, however rich, are never enough.

It is not uncommon for fundamental discoveries in one field to be made by men from other disciplines. The unfettered outsider is still willing to ask himself questions that the expert has accustomed himself by past experience no longer to ask. In a case that contradicts his traditional knowledge the expert often cannot perceive the unusual but critical question. It is important for every manager to know whether he may be afraid of starting what clever (but often short-sighted) men consider to be stupid inquiries and, if so, why.[3]

The program assumed that in management as in medicine, personal integration might be significantly achieved by knowing one's own responses to real situations. It regarded as insufficient, though not as unnecessary, all dialectic about or simulations of reality, such as in-basket exercises, case studies, management games, role-playing and workshop strategems, however rich, detailed, and laborious, because they have already been prefabricated in some predisposing intellectual mold that is not the manager's own. Moreover, to discuss with other students, all equally lacking responsible involvement in any real situation, the manuscript of some unknown third party, is very different from an obligation to act upon one's own impressions of reality. It is for each particular decision-maker to trace the perceptual profiles that his own personal qualities impress upon reality; in practical affairs, his task will never be assigned to him as a package of jig-saw pieces, selected and shaped in the intellectual workshop of another. It will be for him first to sort the amorphous reality into elements that he alone can conveniently manipulate, not least to help him guess what may be on the wrong or missing pieces. Indeed, the medical schools have already grasped this point, for no university has yet proposed to replace its hospital beds and their patients by duplicated files of case notes for students to argue out, by textbook rules and scholastic models, with their professors. Students must still make the primary observations directly on the patients themselves, and, preferably, while they are still alive and in hope of salvation.

An educational policy, therefore, must contrive that the manager, like the clinician, will develop a skill in asking specific questions relevant both to himself and to each unique and unstructured situation. The development of this diagnostic skill is possible only if the managers seeking it are, like the doctors in the medical school, brought into direct and responsible contact with open-ended cases having no approved answers. They must attack the current problems of the enterprise and meet realistically, if not always successfully, the challenge that the unknown makes, not only to their technical knowledge, but also to their non-intellectual qualities.

Thus there were three main parties necessary to this course: the participants, called fellows, who were given the opportunity to examine in detail their own managerial styles; a number of supporting enterprises, most of whom also sent fellows, who provided the strategic opportunities necessary for the participants both to examine and to develop their own managerial styles; and the university staff, whose primary task was to suggest the program of study and research under which these styles could be analyzed and, perhaps, improved.

The Essential Program

The fellows, after their selection[4] approximately six months before the formal start of the program in September, 1968, were each allocated to a personal tutor at one of the five university centers. This tutor first advised each participant how, either by reading or by written exercises, to reach and maintain the academic standard thought necessary for entering the formal scheme. This was composed of a two-month introductory course, a three-month diagnostic phase, a month-long visit to America, and a four-month action phase. Each fellow became acquainted with certain cognitive ideas germane to his own management action; he acquired operational skill (insofar as he did not already have it) in the use of these ideas; he developed, in particular, some acquaintance with his own learning processes; and he was assigned to a full-time field study, lasting eight months, of a policy problem in an enterprise *other than his own.* This project may have ranged from helping his supporting enterprise to assess the possibility of a new process (such as to install a computer) to the identification of some better use of a firm's critical assets. One enterprise posed the simple question "Where are we going?"

The fellow's share in such a field study may have helped install the computer more effectively or, on the other hand, to convince the firm that it should be devoting its time and money to projects more urgent than improved data processing, such as finding out what the processed data are, or might be, used for.[5] Either way, the outcome of his project as such was not, at the outset, seen as the primary aim of his participation.

Any exercise was first intended merely to offer the participant an opportunity to examine his own field behavior and his influence on the host enterprise. In practice, the interactions of some participants with the companies to which they were assigned became so resonant that their catalyzing effect on the enterprise in the long term will probably be significantly more powerful than their learning effects on the participants. At frequent intervals each fellow, along with a few of his colleagues, the teaching staff, and representatives of the supporting enterprises, examined the progress of his field activities, using the cognitive ideas he had previously acquired. During the three months of diagnosis, his first aim was to produce trial recommendations for action on some facet of his exercise; the importance of this lay in the opportunity it gave to examine not only the substance of his proposals but also his ostensible reasons for making them and the reception they met from the host management.[6]

At the end of this diagnostic phase[7] all the fellows visited America for a month to present their reports and recommendations for criticism by independent experts. Ten professors, some from the Sloan School of Management at M.I.T. and others from the Harvard Business School, had already been in correspondence with ten of the fellows whose projects fell in the expert fields of each professor—finance, marketing, data processing, organizational change, corporate strategy, and so forth. Each fellow was allotted half a day to introduce his report before all his colleagues, and to start a dialogue, between fellows and faculty, both particular to his own study and general to the expertise of the professors, as a learning process for all. After these ten presentations at the two schools, some of the remaining fellows presented their reports to the experts of four large American firms: American Telephone and Tele- graph, General Electric, Standard Oil of New Jersey, and International Business Machines. Other fellows offered their projects for comment to specialists from McKinsey's and from Arthur D. Little. In addition to these closely organized sessions, many fellows accepted invitations from other American univer- sities and business firms, including banks and insurance com- panies, to discuss their projects with their faculties or managers.

After this American visit, each fellow was occupied in putting some part of his proposals into effect within the supporting enterprise itself. This highly instructive campaign, lasting four months, was to insure that effective action of some kind would flow from the trial recommendations, and it is the essence of the program. Both the early field studies and the recommen- dations prepared for the American visit at all times kept clearly in view this need for action, and it is in observing this need that the program differed from most other management courses offered by universities.[8] The field studies were therefore realis- tically planned from the start, and there was no room in the program either for excessive theorizing (for example, to optimize some imagined parameter such as an estimated stock level or an approximate batch size), or for excessive objectivity (for example, demanding that, in the interests of good research, fellows be discouraged, in the absence of data, from guessing at what is going on instead of making a scientific study to find out).[9]

During this stage each participant was called upon deliberately to attract and realistically to assess the responses, both positive and negative, of the enterprise to his recommendations. These were sometimes radically changed in his efforts to apply them, but in this he also learned a little about both his own imperfect perceptions of reality and of the unanticipated effects that he might have upon that reality; the university group of fellows into which each fellow was integrated from the start of the program was charged to offer him support during what was frequently a frustrating, if instructive, course of self-recognition. It was of great interest to observe the fellows, all with at least ten years of responsible action-oriented management experience, in their efforts to identify the essential nature of getting things done, as distinct from discussing what ought to be done. During this therapeutic stage, moreover, most participants became more aware of their needs for further theoretical ideas, so that the university staff continued to advise men already motivated on programs of supplementary study.[10] And after each fellow formally finished the program he returned regularly to his university group to examine his experience after re-employment. From time to time he made presentations to the university staff and to his former colleagues about his current tasks seen in the light of the learning processes that were his main interest during the program itself. (See note at the end of this chapter.)

THE SETTING OF THE PROJECTS

The role of each supporting enterprise was to provide the opportunity for a participant to examine, against a suitable background, his individual managerial capacity. This could be exercised in a wide variety of ways, and the projects upon which the fellows exercised them were no less varied. The choice of supporting enterprises was restricted, because the criteria of their suitability were fairly rigorous. The first condition was that the senior management be aware of some feature of its corporate strategy demanding major improvement. The enterprise must also have been willing to offer to a fellow the chance to share or to direct an investigation of the problem, and it must already have demonstrated its intention to do something about it (for example, by a resolution of the board or the provision of money in the budget).

These conditions were cardinal; a clear recognition of need, a willingness to cooperate with the fellow, and a predisposing resolution to act. A fourth condition, that the enterprise estab-

lish a working party[11] specifically to introduce, if not to implement, the recommendations for action, was asked during the
action phase; the deliberations of some of these working
parties have already shown that about two hundred persons
are significantly involved in the changes set in motion by some
of the fellows.

Each enterprise thus proposed and helped to design, with
the university staff and the visiting participant himself, a
project, to fulfil to some degree three conditions: to enable
the participant to examine his own methods of work; to clarify
the enterprise's own problems and suggest the effectiveness of
their possible solutions; and to help the university staff improve
their operational knowledge of management processes.

PROJECT DEVELOPMENT

Nineteen projects were organized for twenty-one fellows,
and two of the projects were double:

Project Number	Receiving Enterprise	Main Theme
1	An international fabric and paper company	To identify the main problems of innovation and of marketing policy
2	The world's largest producer of zinc	To examine critically the information network of the enterprise and to recommend accordingly
3	A major Belgian bank	To examine the changes taking place within the world of banking and the consequent need for the bank to develop a marketing strategy
4	An international producer and seller of wire and of articles based on the technology of wire forming.	To examine the potential of the computer in developing and controlling the operations of the enterprise
5	A major Belgian bank	To examine the incidence of change upon the staff of

		this bank, and to suggest the magnitude and causes of problems facing the introduction of new methods
6	An electricity generating and distributing corporation	To suggest an information service for management, adequate for effective decentralization of the enterprise
7	An international oil company	To help in the introduction of a scheme of management information useful for anticipating change and for controlling operations
8	A large insurance company	To improve the commercial services offered by the enterprise
9	An international producer of electronic apparatus	To examine the organizational problems of a complex assembly system, and to suggest a set of procedures adequate for the procurement and stocking of many component parts
10	A large insurance company	To examine the human and social problems of automatic data processing
11	An international chemical company	To match the principal information streams of the enterprise with its main decision centers
12	An international company that makes, installs and maintains commercial and marine telegraphy systems	To review the system of information now focused around the present computer and to ask how it should be developed
13	An international firm that makes and markets wood products of all kinds	To consider the information and organization useful in the development strategy of principal products
14	A refiner of nonferrous metals, handling the largest annual tonnage of copper in Europe	To consider whether changes in the management structure of the enterprise (notably by increasing

		decentralization of decision-making) is likely to improve the effectiveness with which middle management now uses its abilities
15	An old established and world-famous steel company	To study the transfer and use of information about the needs and potentials of the enterprise for innovation
16	A major producer of steel sheet	To review in detail the conditions for defining, developing and launching (or not launching) a new product
17	An international producer of photographic apparatus and materials of all kinds	To examine the relations between the departments of production, marketing, and finance with reference to the demand for and supply of light sensitive products
18	A large Belgian bank	To examine the potential of the computer for this bank and its probable impact upon the organizational structure
19	An international producer of large-scale civil engineering materials.	To examine the relations between the enterprise and its customers in the light of improved information services.

Several examples of these statements somewhat expanded follow:[12]

Project Number	Extended Summary of Project
3	The main factors of change in Belgium are a challenge to the established supremacy (based on agreed credit rates) of the three large banks, by other national banks, government agencies, private savings banks, and foreign banks. The study of the effect of this competition is made sharper, although not necessarily simpler, by the recent setting up of a marketing

department within the bank; this department has representation at all levels of the bank's structure, although it is not yet clear what influence its staff will have throughout the organization, both regional and local. Thus the total problem is two-sided: to clarify relations between the bank as a whole and its customers as a whole; and to structure the organization internally so as to strengthen these bank-customer relations as much as possible. The study lends itself admirably to a monograph on the new marketing strategies being forced upon an old and traditional financial service, in whatever country it may exist.

4   In the past the computer has been used for traditional data-processing: wages, sales, cost analysis. Some of this has been integrated in a straightforward fashion, and the existing computer is occupied for about two-thirds of its time. It is now desirable to extend the data-processing to the physical operations of wire-production, such as the linking of delivery and of order dates; the advising of the shipping department about completed orders; the control of finished or semifinished products; the allocation of work to machines, and so forth. If such extensions of data-processing are to be made, then changes of organization and procedure and of the allocation of responsibilities may be no less required than the purchase of a large computer. The project aims to examine some of these changes — in the recruitment and training of manpower, in the design of operating systems, in the need for information processing equipment, and so forth — and to suggest where management's critical problems are likely to arise, and on what time scale they are likely to be solved.

6   The corporation is one of the principal generators and distributors of electrical energy in Belgium, with an annual growth rate of 12 per cent; it pursues a policy of strong decentralization, working through a

national headquarters and fifteen management regions. It is also organized in three management divisions, one for production and two for distribution. Managers at each level are responsible for all decentralized services: technical, commercial, financial, and personnel. There is an extensive data-processing system, generally handling accounts and costs, but inadequate for many operational or other management decisions. What is needed is an information system adequate for management effectively to allocate and control its operational decisions between levels and across functions.

8   This large insurance company conducts its business with customers partly through independent agents who may also deal with other companies. The lowest level of full-time staff employed are known as inspectors and are intended to help the independent agents on all branches of insurance. These inspectors therefore deal with a variety of external agents displaying a wide range of motivations, and also with a range of internal technical services offering a variety of contacts. They are, on this account, key members of the staff, and their relations to the existing organization, including its functions of publicity and sales, need careful examination. The project seeks to suggest what types, if any, of changes, as in structure, remuneration or training, would best help to extend and improve relations between the company and its markets.

14   The receiving enterprise refines nonferrous metals in three large plants; it is facing two radical changes at the present moment: innovation in the actual refining processes and a general expansion of most production activities. Thus both the managements and the physical plants show evidence of over-loading that are likely to grow increasingly stressful, and a thoroughgoing analysis of the total enterprise as a system of inputs and outputs is most desirable. Basically the need is to invest, integrate, or expand at

those particular points most likely to ease the total situation within the enterprise as a whole. For this reason a start has been made at the plant levels and a survey of how the operational managers perceive the present deployment of their time and energy is now under way.

15   This is a large steel producing concern with a production-oriented tradition. Many different departments and agencies are concerned with short-term problems of adaptation and adjustment, but fresh thought needs to be given to the integration of ideas and of effort that might lead to long-term changes based on major capital investment, whether in plant or technology. The project is being developed through several stages that are already clearly defined:

1. An interview program among key members of the management
2. The interpretation of these interviews in terms of both an organization chart and a flow system of essential information
3. The response of this organization and of this information flow to certain known and specific attempts at innovation.

The study aimed at identifying the relations within the management critical to the progress of innovating ideas.

In each enterprise, the managing director nominated some responsible subordinate to look after the visiting fellow, and this subordinate was chosen to see the presence of the visitor as of some advantage to him, generally because he was a potential client, already responsible within his own firm for the attack upon the perceived strategic problem. For this reason, the universities arranged preparatory seminars for these subordinates, who were also brought into regular conferences during the field studies, along with the fellows allocated to the university centers.[13]

3.

The participants were senior and experienced men accustomed to working on their own initiative; they were introduced within each supporting enterprise as persons expected to seek information and interviews wherever it was appropriate. Each had soon identified himself with the problem under review, none asked for a change of theme, all had completed their first proposals for action by the end of the diagnostic phase, and most had soon received a number of instructive lessons in the apparent strengths and weaknesses of their hosts.

Because the solution of any operational problems can be successful only when those involved in it are reasonably clear about its nature, one early task of the participant was invariably a synthesis of how the problem was perceived by different members of his host management. All supporting enterprises cooperated adequately to enable the participants to make these reviews, although, not unnaturally, they differed markedly among themselves in willingness to accept their internal contradictions as significant. The aspect of strategic problem definition that aroused the widest general interest among the fellows was the concept of value. Again and again, the diagnoses of the problems turned upon the simple questions, "But what is this enterprise, in the final analysis, trying to do?" "Who, within it, really cares *what* it does," "What, for example, are they striving to offer the customer?" "What is the coalition of key persons who are trying to clarify this offer?" "What does the enterprise see as the key role of innovation and research, to do present things better or to replace present things with new?" "And when this question has found an answer, does anybody really *want* to act upon it?" It seems that the gaps in most enterprises are not in capital finance, production technology, market acumen, and so forth, but in a reluctance to define and to agree upon a clear line of business,[14] especially if change is thereby demanded in the roles or self-images of the top management.

It was always necessary both to narrow and deepen the specific aspect of the problem on which the visiting fellow was to make his recommendations for action. This area was, as far as possible, concerned with several main departments of the enterprise and aimed to involve them all to some degree.[15] Generally, the action demanded setting up a task force to achieve some specific goal; sometimes several task forces were necessary to search for fresh ideas or information, change existing methods of assessment or evaluation, or to improve coordination between departments. Nevertheless, the most effective, as well as the most essential outcome of the deliberations of these task forces or working parties was always the further definition of the questions, "Where is the power in this enterprise?" and "What is it used for?" Because of the specific nature of the first answers to these questions and of the structured recommendations made upon them, the American visit produced a wide range of responses from and contacts with successful practice. One fellow, studying for the first time the problem of banking strategy, made a network of interviews from New England to California. The senior officials of American banks proved more than ready and more than academically interested in discussing their own strategic problems with an action-oriented manager from Europe who did not happen to be a banker. It has become fairly clear that even in the most traditional industries the recommendations of the intelligent outsider, *when framed in specific action terms*, can be a powerful solvent of established and restrictive policies.[16]

THE SUPPORT OF THE UNIVERSITIES

One feature of the program was the integration of the fellows in small groups around their five university centers. This enabled them, against standards of professional effectiveness, individually to compare and contrast among themselves their successes and failures in translating recommendation into action. The origins of the strategic problems facing top management were, in general, so similar from one enterprise to another that the fellows could not fail to learn from discussing each other's progress, especially in communicating among themselves about the communication problems within their hosts. Seldom in the history of management research had twenty experienced men, with the close and interested cooperation of a full-time university staff, simultaneously attacked twenty examples of this basic problem. Their insights should teach us something about both the problems of policy formation and of organizational change.

The staff of these five university centers had several roles, some not traditional for management teachers. Their main responsibility was to help with the design and development of the projects in which the fellows were engaged. In so helping, they themselves were called upon to supply practical advice on sampling, programming, statistical analysis, and questionnaire design, and to introduce fellows to other experts on the university staff able to discuss the many general questions — economic, cultural, technological — that the fellows occasionally confronted. Each member of the staff was expected to act in the traditional role of personal tutor to the four or five participants at his center, especially in advising them on any supplementary reading that they found necessary. Each was also responsible for developing the catechism of cognitive subjects and for engendering an opening balance of operational skills among the participants. Each played an active part in visiting the participants at their supporting enterprises, and in the weekly seminars at which the progress of the participants was examined. Each also acted as a contact between the fellows and any academic research at their own universities, of which the field projects of the fellows provided practical application. The university staff also kept in touch with nominated persons at the supporting enterprises, and discussed from time to time with them, and among themselves, the main implications for management science and other scholarly pursuits, of what was discovered, suggested, or disproved. Perhaps the strongest among the staff were those who saw their role not as teachers but as providers of an opportunity to learn; not as sources of knowledge or information, but as collaborators in the framing of questions and in the sharing of doubts.

Theoretical Foundations of the Program

For managers to perceive their influence on the situations they are trying to manage, they need the opportunities to understand their own imperfect responses to the unstructured situations into which they are necessarily thrust, and the behavior on their own parts that will best help them and their colleagues define the tasks by which they believe themselves to be faced. This will involve them in continuously specifying and amending their supposed objectives, the obstacles that stand in the way of reaching these objectives, and the resources available to remove or reduce the obstacles. This search for corporate strategy will suggest the data they may need to collect; the observations and sources most likely to provide it; its relevance, reliability, and so forth; the evaluation and treatment of these data; and, among much else, the subjective effects that these observations and suggestions produce on those from whom they have collected the data, or with whom they will wish to discuss it. By observing these effects among themselves, the fellows in the program learned how their own behavior affected others, thus enabling them to test their own self-understanding; they could compare their own impressions, conclusions, and actions with those of others; they learned how they and others respond to different attempts to influence and to be influenced; and how differences between persons in the same situation, if intelligently contrasted and compared, can lead to learning and to improved communication.

These ideas, a mixture of scientific method, decision theory, and learning process, were the foundation of the frequent discussions, both at the five university centers and among the fellows assembled as a group, about goals and progress. At no time during the course was there any ex-cathedra teaching of academic principles, and specialized techniques were offered only when asked for, and then to develop the powers of observation and criticism already latent in each fellow.

INTRODUCTORY SYLLABUS

One of the outstanding needs in the education of managers is a frame of reference for describing, communicating, and evaluating the subjective consciousness of personal action. The language of the management academy is a code of depersonalized abstractions, such as economic theory, industrial law, network analysis, quantitative methods, and so forth. But the manager who personally challenges reality must first ask "What view of the me-here-and-now is appropriate in using any of my knowledge?" Although it was the first assumption of this program that only practice will enable the manager to treat this question satisfactorily, nevertheless it is suggested that a way of perceiving six particular subjects will help him to structure his subjective experience better. These subjects, together with practice in interviewing skills, exercises in the design of study projects, discussions to illuminate interpersonal understanding, and similar preparations for a program of inquiry and action, occupied the fellows for the first two months.[17]

The Nature of Values

All management action implies a set of purposes; the manager should be trying to achieve *something*. Thus, those who set out to observe their own managerial behavior should be aware of the general notion of value systems, of things seen as worthwhile, of goals to be striven for, of criteria for identifying them, and of sacrifices to be made in reaching them. (It has already been observed how imperative the fellows felt the need of top management generally to be for such awareness.) Any discussion of value systems raises a host of ideas, from economic utility and the measurement of cash flow, to intuitive judgments made by experts against scales of purely experiential origin.

The Nature of Information

The working material of managers is information, and at all times the fellows concentrated upon its nature and upon the differing managerial uses to which it is put. Incidental methods of sampling; problems of transmitting data through intermediaries whose perceptions of its meaning may transform it in the process; estimates of the value of information to a manager who without it would be obliged to take greater risks: these were a few of the ideas examined. Fellows were greatly impressed both by the problems of getting information to where it should be needed and by the insensitivity of many key managers to the lack of it.

The Logic of Systems

All management activity occurs at a point in time: it is conjured from some previous state of affairs and creates fresh situations in the future. Ideas of flow or transfer, including purpose, delay, storage, loss, transformation, control, and so forth, whether applied to cash, funds, or working capital, or to materials, energy, or information, are cardinal in any analytical approach to the manager's task.

The Theory of Decision

Once values have been provisionally identified, certain decisions need to be taken both to plan and to fulfill the achievement of objectives specific to local conditions. Thus each fellow was informed, before he started his field observations, on the general nature of decisions. It has been possible, with the caliber of participant attracted by the program, not only to discuss with most of them the main elements of any decision, but also the basic ideas of statistical decision theory and the common models of operational research.

The Estimation of Uncertainty

The manager's world is full of uncertainty, not only because reality cannot be foretold, but also because it cannot be accurately known even in the present. Thus ideas of inference from limited data; of statistical significance, suggesting the measurable likelihood of such-and-such a relationship; of concordance, suggesting the amount of agreement between independent subjective judgments; of variance analysis, suggesting some order in much confusion: a minimum acquaintance with all of these was encouraged among the fellows to help them identify the structure of their managerial environment.

Learning and Adaptation

Finally, managers do not change situations without themselves being changed in the process. Managers resistant to new ideas are unlikely to bring about new situations around them. Such interactions are a learning process, although in a culture dominated by books, it is not always appreciated how effectively men learn from their own practical experience. It was fundamental to this program that all managers touched by it should become aware of the nature of their own learning processes. Indeed, there is something to be said for the opinion that the first objective of management education is to acquaint the subject with this awareness.

It may be useful to illustrate the use of these concepts with an example from the program. Say a firm wishes to understand more clearly its experiences both of change and of resistance to change. It is the first task of the fellow, by his practical description of a recent change within the enterprise—or of the recent abortion of some new idea—to identify the perceptions that key persons have of their goals. What do they believe is worth doing and proper for them to do? What aspects of the change do they approve of, or even actively promote? What, if anything, are they against in it, and for what reasons? (What comments on their answers does the fellow himself have to make? What is his own value system in contrast to those of his hosts?). Second, the fellow needs to ask what kinds of information are available to the enterprise. How does the management *know* whether what it is trying to do is, in any sense, in accord with its values and ambitions? How much of what is discussed and reported is genuine information and how much is guesswork? (What information does the fellow himself think the enterprise ought to collect and use?)

Third, through what manner of system or organization does this information flow, and what are the critical points therein? How is this network perceived by those who occupy these critical points? Does the accountant, for example, say that he could measure every item of cost in the production process—

and so advise the manufacturing superintendent on his most economical production methods—if only he were asked? Or does the manufacturing superintendent say that because he is a master of all known production methods, if the accountant would give him the detailed costings of his present processes, he could very soon bring his factory expenditure to an absolute minimum without in any way sacrificing quality? (How does the fellow himself see this critical obstruction to change? What advice should he give the accountant or the manufacturing superintendent? What should be their places in any task force? How will he convey his views to the president?)

Fourth, given such gaps in the transfer of critical information, what kind of decisions are or can be made? What, indeed, is the nature of the decision necessary to close these system gaps? What ought to be the key decisions necessary for launching, or intelligently opposing, some proposed innovation? What are, or should be, the criteria of its acceptance or rejection? How are the various parties brought together to agree on their opportunities and on their strengths? (How does the fellow see his own part in this decision process? What has been made possible by his intervention? Does he prepare the management to take decisions that in his absence they would not have taken? What is his catalyzing role?)

Fifth, what are the principal areas of risk and uncertainty in the management system? Are they of two kinds: those of inherent uncertainty and those created by the management itself? How are the second kind eliminated? What kind of information shortages create the first? How far can research overcome them? In the total risk, what factors are most relevant? How far do different members of the management estimate differently the risks involved? Is it possible to reduce the total risk by comparing and contrasting the different estimates of it made by different experts? (What does the fellow think the risks are? What does he feel about the attitudes of the management toward them? Are some too rash? Are others too cautious? For what reasons? What set of arguments would the fellow set out in a written judgment of the risk, should the president invite him to submit one, and what experience from outside the project would he bring to drawing up his case?) Finally, to what extent will the project, by this first involvement of the management in clarifying their values, tracing their information flows, discovering the gaps in their organization, structuring better their decisions, and assessing more accurately their present risks, help the management to deal more effectively with some second or future major issue?

The present exercise, concerned with understanding innovation, will not illuminate all the troubles likely to torment the management, either now or henceforth. But if, having worked systemically through one strategic question with the help of a visiting fellow, the enterprise will be better equipped to tackle a second — such as to match better the decision system with the information system — it can be said that true learning has taken place.[18] (How does the fellow see the project as a lesson for himself? As he reads back to his early formulations of its design and of its action stages, can he identify how immature his first impressions of it were? What were the main influences bringing about these changes in his own perception of the issues? What relevance to his own tasks does he see in this experience as a change agent in another enterprise?)

CONCLUSION

The essence of the Inter-University Program in Belgium is that management education — whatever it may already be doing to spread general principles by approved syllabuses to selected classes of students — must now also make a decisive and structured attempt to examine, understand, and improve the actions of unique managers faced with unique situations. A code is needed for understanding the apparently critical and the fortuitous. This program thus challenged and accepted the action needs of the real world rather than avoided or underrated them. Fortune and misfortune, jackpot and take-over, windfall and crisis, as much as any routinely perfected principles of management, determine the course and progress of the enterprises on which they descend.

The slender syllabus of the program may well be a reflection of our own ignorance, for we know little enough about personal uniqueness and not much more about the responses of complex systems to random stress. Nevertheless, there may be rewards for our persistence in examining what is real; for asking what imperfect and inadequate individuals actually do rather than what the noblest of humanity would like others to do; for looking at the firm as it exists rather than arguing about some model of it; for studying what happens in practice rather than in theory. Although the first objective was always to help the individual fellow better use his existing talents, there are also potential gains to the enterprises and even to the universities in this less ambitious, if not admittedly unimaginative, approach.

NOTES

1. In reply to the question "Am I my brother's keeper?" there are some who may emphatically say, "No." A professor, for example, cannot be obliged to take responsibility for the bankruptcy of an ex-student who failed by trying to implement the theory of the firm or to apply the principles of marginal utility. This responsibility remains with the ex-student alone. It was not always so: Cleopatra was said to have had her tutor flogged every time she played a wrong note upon her flute. It is also common for sports teams to fire their managers or coaches after a poor season.

2. The personality of each manager and the singularity of every strategic problem that confronts him are alike, by their very uniqueness, variations on the general laws of human behavior and of management theory (such as those laws may be). On this account, the particular qualities of individual men and the once-for-all details of irrecoverable events necessarily tend to be overlooked, or even deliberately rejected by, the scientist in his search for order and for generality. H. A. L. Fisher, however, abandoned this scholarly mission and saw history merely as one wave of emergency succeeding another. But management education, drawing largely upon university thought and teaching, still expresses an overriding belief in the study of general principles; the examination of critical events and of exceptional behavior as the springs of management action in their own right still lies largely in the future. Perhaps the universities of Belgium are here making one attempt to start it.

3. The classical myth is that of David and Goliath; only David among the Israelites was inexpert enough to see that in the new situation the proper question was not "Where do we find a stronger man?" but "Given that we have no stronger man, what new weapon do we take against Goliath?" It is said that Bismarck had the greatest mistrust of experts, whom he found invariably to be misinformed, especially when trying to put their own subject into a wider perspective.

4. The selection procedure was simplicity itself. Fellows were asked to write a short essay on what they imagined the course mainly would do for them. Any who looked eagerly forward to learning techniques, such as PERT, CPM, DCF, or FIFO, were at once rejected. This was a program set up mainly to learn a little about themselves.

5. Some details of the projects are given on page 12. Each was an attack on a strategic question; that is, one influencing the future of the firm, but also critically bound up with the value system of its key managers.

6. Although there were specific provisions that no firm would attempt to hire the visiting fellow who worked on their projects, it has been made known to certain fellows that their host enterprises would be receptive of any proposals to continue a close association with their guests now the full-time projects have terminated.

7. It would be unreal to assume that diagnoses and therapy can be as sharply divided as this timetable suggests.

8. The Oxford program organized by Mr. Norman Leyland draws upon similar ideas, although most participants work on the problems of their own enterprise.

9. The capacity to reflect upon his own guessing proclivities might well be among a risk-taker's most precious assets.

10. Some of the staff, reciprocally, have seen their own need to learn from the participants.

11. The nature of any such working party must be determined during the diagnostic phase. It must vary from one enterprise to another, and must depend on the definition and development of its project. One of the early tasks of each fellow was to identify the clients within his supporting enterprise, as distinct from the top management who offered the project. It was for the fellow to coordinate, in his role as change agent, the interests and energies of all those likely to be affected by his recommendations.

12. These were written during the diagnostic phase and as the projects developed into action they were certainly seen differently by those who worked on them.

13. In any future program a major aim must be to develop the contact between university center and supporting enterprise, using the fellow as the agent.

14. My experience with management information systems in Britain illuminates the same problem somewhat differently. Here the sense of competition between rival firms is so keen that at times it occupies the entire attention of top management. Managing directors seem like athletes on a track, so absorbed in watching each other for sudden sprints that they have almost forgotten what race they are in. Professors of related subjects are sometimes even more alert to anticipating the movements of their colleagues.

15. Experience of the projects seems to suggest that success in promoting change depends on the resolution of an obvious paradox: action must be specific at a particular point by a particular individual, although its effects will be felt generally by all whose tasks interact with that of the individual initiating the action. The successful change is that in which the effects of highly specific action are well integrated into more general practice, and it is in this integration that the quality of communications within the enterprise plays a decisive part. (See also p. 90).

16. A simple recommendation for feasible action may have the most singular effect upon particular boards of management. So long as there is no serious intention to act upon a report, it will be received with the greatest enthusiasm and unanimity; only when the path to practical action is opened is any danger seen to arise. This is because praising reports demands only eloquence, whereas taking action upon them calls for commitment.

17. We need rigorous ways of assessing whether this time was usefully spent; suggestions about the evaluation of the entire program have been accepted for any second trial. In the meantime, a provisional assessment has been made of the first by a university department not concerned with its design and organization.

18. If the enterprise has truly learned, its key managers are in a better position to take strategic decisions. These demand information about the external environment in which the enterprise exists, information about the resources available internally to the management and a realistic perception of management's own value system, including its motivating drives. In my view— shared by the majority of the fellows—the program has probably improved most this understanding of management's own inner responsibility to decide what it wants to do.

2

Theoretical Guidelines

When a score of managers, each at the meridian of his professional life, are persuaded to invest a year in examining their professional styles, it is prudent to define the strategy of such examination. At least it should be clear about where to start. For even if it is manifestly difficult to foresee all that is likely to happen when twenty senior managers are interchanged in order that each may study a strategic problem in one of nineteen enterprises other than his own, these developments are bound to be influenced by any ideas on which their studies are first encouraged to draw. Many experimental methods are available; fellows were certainly advised to sample the literature of psychological and social inquiry, economic and financial analysis, quantitative methods, operational research, and so forth. Throughout their year, moreover, they were encouraged to keep in touch with university staff experts, and the internal structure of the program was so contrived that each fellow could also make his own professional knowledge readily available to others.

However, a sufficiency of technical and analytical method is not enough. A model of strategic action is called for, a framework simple enough and flexible enough for twenty powerfully motivated fellows to employ in ordering and in bartering their different experiences. In constructing such a model before the program started, it seemed that three conditions had to be satisfied: that the fellows were to learn from their experience; that this experience was to include both the diagnosis and treatment of a real problem; and that this problem was to be strategic, or concerned with the total enterprise in its economic and social setting.

The first of these required that the program draw upon some theory of learning; the second that the program include a paradigm merging observation and analysis with action and control; the third that it integrate the environment of the enterprise with its inner capacities, including the subjective qualities of the strategists themselves. Another desirable condition appeared to be that the separate expression of these three elements would enable them readily to find expression as an integrated whole. It should also be possible to use the integrated model for deploying without undue difficulty the traditional methods of specialized research.

The model chosen from the outset was a systemic integration of three subsystems: system alpha, of the design of a strategy; system beta, of the negotiation of the strategy so designed; and system gamma, of the learning process of the strategists involved.

As the projects developed, the theoretical system generated a crop of extremely concrete questions; it also began to suggest ways of structuring the behavior of individuals so as partly to account for their success or failure as managers. It is thus anticipated that should the program ever be repeated the original theoretical model, as it became enriched with the practical experience of these pioneer fellows, will serve as an opening guide.[1] In the meantime, it seems to offer scope enough for improvement, not only to correspond more with the needs of this particular management program, but also as an aid in the development of a general theory of human action. The search for a science of praxeology, identified by Espinas in 1896, has not attracted the attention given to the more traditional sciences;[2] the present attempts to understand better the control and consequences of human behavior in structured organizations, however, should help this search. A general model should then be useful, not only for laying out the chessboard of the managerial strategist, but also for describing the success or failure of ordinary persons attempting to do ordinary things.

No enterprise makes up its impersonal mind about where to go or what to do—nor does it automatically set out to do it or to get there—simply because it has no impersonal mind to make up. Its behavior as a total entity is largely determined by the most powerful coalition inside it. This is generally, but not always, the board of directors representing the top management of the enterprise. It may happen, on the other hand, that the effective power is not in the board taken as a whole, but in a caucus of two or more members; again, it may not be within the top management at all, but in some unofficial league of key executives out in the field of operations. It may occasionally lie with the trade union to which the employees of the enterprise belong. Factional or internecine war, even anarchy, are also not unknown.

However this may be, in managerial terms and in a competitive economy, it can be said that the first voluntary preoccupation of this power group should be a continuous review of its goals; and that its second is the direction of the enterprise toward them. (In a competitive world one of these goals may be the maintenance of the winning coalition itself, or at least of its power to nominate successors.) These two main tasks are here to be identified as, first, a process of design, and second, a process of negotiation. Because design is largely an intellectual process, and because negotiation is largely a temperamental process, and also because intellectual and emotional qualities are independent, it follows that first-class managers are rare. They need exceptional endowment in two unrelated particulars. A good negotiator, poor at design, is often behind every bad plan well-carried-out (Goethe's "Ignorance in Motion").

In addition to a mastery of the two elements of design and of negotiation, in a changing world a successful management must also bring to its work the capacity to benefit from its experience of that work; it can no longer afford to be expert in yesterday's business. Those who would influence the world about them must, in their turn, be influenced by the world.[3] Thus, in examining the work of top managers and for devising with them programs of education, three principal influences must be considered: the design of strategic objectives or of corporate influences, the execution of these plans in the conditions of everyday operations, and the development of the managers as individuals under the constant stress of devising and carrying out their strategies.

THE BASIC NATURE OF ORGANIZATION

Seen from the point of view of the top management (or other coalition of power), every enterprise is a collection of tasks to be done, of opportunities to be grasped, or of problems to be solved. The major problems are those of strategy, to determine where the enterprise is to go and how it is to get there; the secondary problems are those of tactics, to contrive that the resources of the enterprise are reasonably well deployed to meet the demands of strategy; the tertiary problems are those of technology, to ensure that the physical operations are adequate to accomplish the tactical plans so laid down. These three levels may be reflected in the published procedures or in the financial codes of the enterprise. For example, the strategic plan may be expressed in a capital budget spread over several years; the tactical negotiations to carry the plan out may be programmed through an interlocking array of operating budgets; and the control of the technical processes may be surveyed by some system of standard-cost accounting.

More generally, organization is first the process of allocating these tasks, opportunities, and problems to the persons best qualified, either alone or in cooperation with others, to identify and to handle them. The qualifications of any particular person to solve problems depend upon many separate factors, of which a majority seem to be determined, not by the person himself, but by the system of which he is part. However, organization may also be the process of distributing information about tasks, opportunities, and problems so that those who tackle them may learn from their experience in doing so. It is the central thesis of this book that in the present epoch of tumultuous change, an urgent need of every enterprise, and of every key person within it, is to learn from his experience of today how both to anticipate and to enact better his experience of tomorrow. It must therefore be ensured that personal and social learning develop from the daily task, and are not seen only as the specific and exclusive responsibility of some adventitious organ of the business enterprise, such as a training department. Much less should this capacity to identify, accept, and influence the accelerating stream of events be thought of as the exclusive product of a management development course; not a little traditional organization theory, for example, if acted upon inside the normal enterprise, would probably produce results very different from those anticipated by its advocates.[4]

INFORMATION AND RISK

Within any given organization the persons best qualified, at any given moment, to solve a tangled problem, or to seize a profitable chance, are those who need the least information, the least energy and the least materials for doing so. Information is needed to identify both the nature of the task to be performed and of the means of performing it; energy and materials are necessary for taking action. Insofar as a manager has to perform tasks for which his information is incomplete, he must take risks, and the magnitude of any risk is directly measurable from this information gap. A manager may, by searching and analyzing, gradually reduce the information gap, but events may overtake him, so that he is obliged to deal with his task, and to guess about a course of action, knowing that at the time he has insufficient information about both its desirable objectives and its economical operations. Thus the usefulness of extra information can often be measured by the lessening of attendant risk, and even a specific value given to any particular message. Against this value must be set the cost of transmitting the message, including the collection of the data that goes into it. The ideal organization is that which derives the greatest value from the messages it is capable of generating. Those who control the communication system must therefore be aware of the classes of problems they are called upon to solve and of the information most relevant to their solution; they must also know where the relevant information can be found and where it should be brought to bear. The following pages set out the classes of questions suggesting what relevant information should be available.

An organization that is economical at one moment in the generation and transmission of messages useful to decision makers may be less economical at some later time. A network both transparent and intelligible in an epoch of parchment and quill pens may not readily be suitable for electronic data processing. But possibly it can be adapted to such use; and the need for adaptation, or for personal and institutional learning, is continuous. We must on that account contrive that our systems of information and decision have built into them some quality of continuous adaptation. If the gaps in the systems for collecting and distributing information are so great that managers are unwilling continuously to take risky decisions, they are unable to learn from observing the outcomes of those decisions. They see only the consequences of their own inactivities, from which no effective learning can occur (see p. 109); thus the capacity of an organization not only to act, but also to develop, is strongly dependent upon the quality of its communications.

The three principal influences on management may thus be represented by systems based on the use of information. We call them system alpha—the use of information for designing objectives; system beta—the use of information for achieving those objectives; system gamma—the use of information for adapting to experience and to change.

ASPECTS OF DESIGN: SYSTEM ALPHA

A decision is a declaration, whether explicit or not, by a particular manager to undertake some course of action. His course of action, to be feasible, demands, first that he value what he anticipates will be the outcome of the action; second, that he be aware of the external difficulties he will need to surmount in order to achieve this outcome; and third, that he can find internal resources enough to deal with these difficulties at a cost consonant with the value of the outcome. As the foregoing arguments imply, he must have adequate[5] information about these three components (values, externals, and internals) of a feasible course of action. Every decision to ward off trouble, or to resolve problems, thus demands information for answering these three questions: What is my fear of loss? What is the occasion of it? What can I do about it?

If the managerial task is taken positively, that is, not as overcoming troubles but as grasping opportunities, the three questions become What am I hoping to win? What is the particular chance I am now offered for winning it? How do I make the most of this chance?

In general, these are the key questions of the entrepreneur, of the businessman, of the board of directors of every enterprise trying to secure its present success and its future growth. In practical terms, the questions demand that every manager or board of management explore three sets of ideas. In classical decision theory they reflect the elements first, of utility, choice, preference (managerial values); second, of problem, opportunity, state of nature (external system); and third, of resources, actions, means (internal system). More specific questions, about any particular decision, include the following.

Managerial Values[6]

What are the value systems of those who have the greatest power in the decision? What do they believe in? What, among their various beliefs, are their priorities? What do they most want to achieve? What are their own life goals? What fateful forces do they feel at work on them that they must obey? What are their economic utilities? Do they wish to found new industrial dynasties or to add further luster to those from which they descend? What are their social constraints or expectations? What significant differences of value exist among these central decision takers? How (if at all) are these differences made explicit? How are they resolved or accommodated?

The External System

What, more explicitly, is the nature of the problem now being faced, or of the opportunity now being offered? Who will buy, or accept, the products of the decision? What is the further market for the efforts of the entrepreneur? Who are his existing customers? What do they come to him for? Who is now the ultimate consumer of the products? What are the needs, *external to the decision-maker*, upon satisfying which his efforts continue to depend for their viability? Is there a distinction between the distribution channel and the customers themselves? Are these customers also the ultimate consumers? For how long and with what intensity is the external demand going to last? Who else does or can supply it? What, if anything, is likely to replace it?

The Internal System

What is the capacity of the entrepreneur to satisfy the demand? What does it cost him to do so? What total resources does he already command that he may bring to bear upon supplying the market? Which resources does he use well? Why are others not used so well? What authority has he to secure more resources? What unused capacity of any kind is available to him? What can he do to exploit its potential? Indeed, what precisely is this internal system over which, as its boss, he has a significant power? What, in particular, fixes its limits and influences its growth?

In colloquial terms, the three sets of questions could be summarized by a board of directors asking themselves: What makes any of us care about our business (management values)? Where have we now got to in this world (external system as perceived)? Who do we all think we are (internal resources as perceived)?

Thus the design of a management decision, or of that set of latent decisions generally called a strategy, demands information about three critical elements: the value system of the managers, the external system that they exploit, and the internal system by which they exploit it. The structured interplay of these three sets of information, here called system alpha, is the design process of a management decision. With adjustments between the values of local managers and those of their superiors, and between the scopes of the internal and external systems appropriate to different levels of management, system alpha is universal. Managers at all levels, from company presidents to assistant charge hands, must first design (or be helped to design) their decisions in accordance with system alpha.

It may be suggested that the critical difference between strategy formation in American and in European business lies in the American emphasis on the external system. Not until the market has been thoroughly examined are the production plans elaborated; efficient though the American engineer may be, it is from the merchant that he takes his instructions. It is this obedience to the commands of the market that dictates the universal use of management by objectives, which in turn calls for the support of electronic data processing.

The system alpha paradigm is the basis of many operational research models, particularly those based on the decision theories of Abraham Wald, or the more traditional theorems of allocation and delay. Given that indications of particular external conditions, or states of nature, are reliable to particular extents, and given that particular states of nature respond to particular treatments (use of resources) with statistically known utilities, it is possible to suggest what resources should be deployed against what indications, that is, to settle the best strategies for handling particular sorts of puzzles. That such decision theory may be of severely limited practical use does not destroy its considerable theoretical interest in helping one to think strategically in terms of system alpha. It is no purpose of this book, however, to discuss the technologies of decision making, nor the many mathematical models built on structured interactions among the three sets of information identified under system alpha. Such technologies are the professional concern of operational research, and as such need not be among the working equipment of top managers. However, to recognize the three elements of system alpha, and to trace them in any decision situation whatever, are cardinal tasks for every person carrying responsibility for the work of others.[7]

decision maker	decision values	external system	internal system
primitive savage	satisfy hunger	jungle creatures	bow and arrows
factory worker	increase earnings	good jobs elsewhere	employable skills
production foreman	meet deadline	human problems	theory X or theory Y
factory owner	maximise sales volume	customer needs	men and machinery
research laboratory	enhance reputation	unsolved problems	scientific tradition
board of directors	ensure growth	rivals and suppliers	take-over power
immature nation	military glory	weak neighbours	bigger guns
operatic soprano	popular appeal	television audiences	voice and publicity

FIGURE 1 — Showing typical, but oversimplified, system alpha elements for certain decision makers.

The single entries in each cell are, of course, inadequate to represent any reality . The primitive savage does not want only to satisfy his hunger; he wishes to preserve his own life, and he may also want the skin of any beast he kills to keep himself warm. His resources include more than his weapons, particularly if he decides to cooperate with other savages. On the other hand, his external system is fairly described, though his quarry may change from season to season and from place to place.

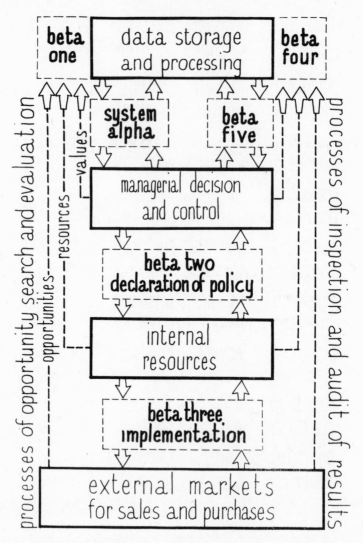

FIGURE 2—Showing emergence of system beta as a consequence of applying system alpha for the attainment of valued objectives, by the application of internal resources to external opportunities.

This is a little more elaborate than Figure 1, and it is instructive to employ on

Aspects of Negotiation: System Beta

Decisions can be designed or strategies elaborated in terms of system alpha only after information about the situation has been secured; the practical value of the design must be tested by how the decision then stands up to influencing the situation itself. Both the antecedent stage of data collection, and the subsequent development of the selected design through attempts to use it, are essential phases in the negotiation aspects of every management task. The cycle of negotiation, here called system beta, is as follows:

1. A survey stage, in which data on the three design elements of system alpha are identified
2. A trial decision stage, in which a first design, using system alpha, is selected[8] from among a number of alternative designs

---

any of the entries thereof. The savage, for example, would first reflect upon his hunger, not perhaps at great depth, although if it were mixed with other needs, such as to feed unexpected guests or to reline the floor of his hut, he might spend some time on agreeing with friends what their needs (values) were and what was their order of priority. In a culture where weapons take long to make, the hunter might count over with care his available resources; and his estimates of where the game might be and of how hard he would find the task of stalking it would not be frivolously attained. Hence his stage of survey (beta one) would be clearly identifiable; it might, in fact, when merged with the stage of provisional decision (beta two) be highly ritualised, with sacrifices, ceremonial fires and dances, every bit as definite as the banquets celebrating the decision of an English shipping company to spend a lot of other peoples' money on resuscitating Edwardian sea travel. The savage's stage of action (beta three) would include tracking his quarry, and it would be intermingled with his stage of inspection (beta four), continually looking out for prints to show whether the beast had in fact recently passed that way. Since each arrow would be precious, he would note with great care where, in case of a miss, he had shot the last one; if the beast he was after left a track unexpectedly crossed by that of a tiger he would bear this well in mind and perhaps, on this evidence of beta four, reconsider his next moves in beta three. (He might even, there and then, return to beta two and thereon, through beta five, give up the search). Sooner or later he would need to decide, through beta five, whether to carry on, to change his strategy or to abandon it. And if the original programme demanded a mixed bag, he would need to check, from time to time, how far he was towards filling it. Thus the system beta paradigm is capable of describing even the most out-of-the-way activities.

3. An action stage, in which the trial design is implemented, either in whole or in part, either in reality or in some simulated form

4. An inspection or audit stage, in which the observed outcome of the action stage is compared with the outcome expected when the first design was selected[9]

5. A control stage, in which appropriate follow-up action is taken on the conclusions drawn from the inspection (Such conclusions will be to confirm, modify, or reject the first design; or to repeat the cycle of negotiation in the light of experience gained from its first application.)

A moment's reflection will show that system beta flows directly from any attempt to employ system alpha, that is, to take action enabling the subject to achieve a more desirable grasp of his environment. In Figure 2 the four levels represent, from the bottom up, a situation of industrial management in this order:

1. The relation of the decision maker to the external system, namely to offer finished products or to purchase further resources

2. The relation of the decision maker to the internal system, namely, to command certain resources suitable, if desired, to produce for the external system

3. The relation of the decision maker to his own value system, enabling him to decide what to produce with what resources

4. A symbolic representation of the information processing system at the disposal of the decision maker

The flow diagram that is Figure 2 suggests that the first process (beta one) is to assemble information about the external and the internal systems and about the management values. From this, a first processing operation results in a provisional decision (beta two) in the form of a statement to the internal system. This results in action (beta three) upon the external system; the effects of this are fed back or audited (beta four), bringing fresh information, or knowledge of results, into the consideration of management; this will decide whether or not to proceed along the same lines again (beta five).

It is clear that system beta can appear in many forms, from the decision made at his desk by a solitary manager, who believes himself already to know what is needed to secure the cycle of negotiation, to the formation of the international strategies of a world enterprise over a period of many years. Collecting and classifying data, using such data to make plans, trying out the plans, auditing the results of them and, in consequence, rejecting or improving the plans have been the occupation of mankind for countless generations. There are, in fact, seven references to the process of audit or inspection in the very first chapter of Genesis.

The system beta paradigm is of great interest; it is the structure, not only of the negotiation aspects of a decision, but also of the general learning process (see p. 105) and of the scientific method. In the latter the five stages become

1. A stage of observation, in which the scientist assembles data relevant to his chosen field of scientific knowledge (His genius is indicated by the width of relevance that he is able to handle.)
2. A stage of hypothesis or theory, from which he conjectures or infers a set of relations inside his data (Again his genius is indicated, even more powerfully, by his ability to suggest relations between data not previously thought of as connected, e.g., that the force pulling the apple to the ground is also the force keeping the moon in its orbit.)
3. A stage of experiment, in which is carried out a set of practical tests, designed impartially to determine whether or not the hypothesis is likely to be correct (The design of these tests may tax the technical skill of the scientist severely; he cannot, for example, contrive direct experiments in astronomy.)
4. A stage of inspection, in which the observed results of the experiment are compared with those predicted by the hypothesis when the tests were designed (It is not unknown for experimental results to appear to prove the hypothesis

exactly, when further analysis of the meaning of the results shows that an alternative or opposing hypothesis is equally probable; the Balmer series was once taken as the final proof of the Rutherford-Bohr model of the atom but only a decade later as proof of Schrödinger's wave-mechanics model.)

5. A stage of consolidation, in which the outcome of the four previous stages is first scrutinized and then related to the whole body of previously relevant knowledge; the hypothesis is either confirmed, modified and re-examined, or it is rejected (Some hypotheses remain long in a state of suspended judgment, because of experimental difficulties that inhibit the production of convincing evidence one way or the other; one such example was the nature of lunar craters.)

Specialization

In many large enterprises seen as complete organisms the five stages of system beta become represented by specific managerial functions or even by specialist professional departments. Some of these are shown in Figure 3.

The managerial treatment within each of the five specialized stages of system beta must also repeat system beta itself. If we consider only the first stage – that of observation, or of collecting enough reliable facts about, say, the market – we must proceed as follows:

1. Survey: collect sample of data at random from a given universe and classify it.
2. Trial decision: on the basis of these data, suggest some relationship or hypothesis.
3. Action: collect fresh sample of data from the same universe.
4. Inspection: test by statistical means whether the relationship or hypothesis built from the first sample is confirmed by the second.
5. Control: if confirmed, assume that the suggested relationship or hypothesis is valid; if not confirmed, either

system beta

1 survey	2 decision	3 action	4 audit	5 control
market research	product variety	flow process balancing	inventory control	⇨
sales income analysis	pricing policy	discounts and credits	distribution cost analysis	
historical cost data	value analysis	work measurement	standard costing	confirmation, amendments or rejection of decision in light of experience ⇨
personnel records	accident prevention	safety committee	factory inspector	

FIGURE 3 – Showing typical institutionalized or functional aspects of system beta in large organization.

A manufacturing organization does well to survey its potential markets (beta one) and as a result of this to settle upon the variety of products it thinks it well to make (beta two). Thereafter it must give attention, among other things, to the flow of work through its manufacturing shops (beta three) and introduce a system to control the amount of money tied up in semi-finished work (beta four). From time to time, it should review how all this balances and, if necessary, do something about it (beta five) at the policy level.

group leadership = system beta

stage	inputs	outputs
survey	listening questioning	informing explaining
decision	discussing suggestions	agreeing and allocating tasks
action	encouraging initiative	rewarding effort providing support
audit	investigating complaints	reviewing and verifying results
control	conferring to improve general methods following particular experience	

FIGURE 4 — Showing application of system beta to task of group leadership.

The leader of a group may (or may not) have been given a set of objectives to reach, but he will not know his resources fully nor be able to foresee all the problems that his group will encounter. On the second and third elements of system alpha, therefore, he will be obliged to collect information as he goes ahead. This depends upon communication with his group as well as with any higher sources of authority. Moreover, apart from providing a fresh fund of information about his internal and external systems, members of his group re-examine the data or reject the proposed relationship or hypothesis.

In the same way, any of these five steps must themselves be capable of test by system beta, because the processes of verification must be applicable to every detail, even if, in practice, it would be a waste of time to apply such tests.[10]

Thus, the use of system beta, of conjecture and refutation (to use Karl Popper's phrase), proceeds indefinitely, like a recurring decimal or a continued fraction, and logically it does as well in rational management behavior as in the experimental methods of scientific research. Shortage of time may often limit its application in detail; it should never reject it in principle.

---

may be able to help with the design of system alpha itself. Thus a group leader should see his relations with his team in the light of the system beta paradigm. The set of questions, each one of them opening up exchanges between superior and subordinate, to be asked from time to time by any chairman of a meeting are as follows:

survey: what is this situation we are in and how did it arise? let me ask you first and then I will tell you what I know.

decision: what can we do about it? I had an idea that we could try X, but there must be alternatives; how would any of you feel about the part you could play?

action: now we are actually started, what further ideas has anybody got for improving our attack? is there anything you would like me to do to help you get on with your job?

audit: can we discuss what seems to some of us a serious breakdown in the original plan? we are quite a long way from where we ought to be according to the programme, and some of you probably feel that I should have done something about it before now.

control: Now that we have managed to struggle through this job and get it out on the day before we said we would — though I do not yet know at what extra cost — what lessons have we learned for the future?

or

I think it was clear two months ago that the job was going to be a dead loss, and now we have come to the point; I shall have to tell the firm to write it off, but I think we ought to have an inquest and learn what we can about where things went wrong.

or

You do not all need me to tell you that the job went well from the very start. Everything seems to have worked: costs, deadlines, supplies — nothing could go wrong. On this form, it is clear that here is a line we could be good at. Nevertheless, if it seems so easy could we not even do still better?

Supervisory Behavior

The behavior of a man in charge of others, namely, leading them toward the achievement of some objective by means of recurring cycles built on the system beta paradigm, will display two sets of informational exchanges with them, inputs from his group back to the leader, outputs from the leader forward to the group. The behavioral activities through which these information exchanges are effected are suggested in Figure 4.

In a survey conducted among several hundred operatives in Manchester factories,[11] there was frequent reference, by the workers during the free interviews on which the survey was based, to the topics reflected in Figure 4. These were then typified by actual statements, characteristic of management styles, as follows:

1. Capacity to listen (survey): "It's no good trying to get them to listen to you here: you may as well knock your head against a brick wall."
2. Capacity to invite ideas (decision): "If the boss wants anything done here, he generally wants us to put up ideas."
3. Capacity to motivate (action): "Although we seem to have a lot of trouble from time to time, we have to admit that management is always fair in the end."
4. Capacity to review (audit): "You can warn a foreman until you're blue in the face, but nothing is done to prevent your trouble."

According to confidential and noncollusive opinion on these four statements, scattered at random through a questionnaire composed of forty-one different statements, relevant to their work in the factory, the workers were ranked by satisfaction, or lack of it. Marks per statement varied from $+2$ to -2 on a five-point scale. Totals thus varied from $+8$ to -8 on the four statements, and were collected among 266 different individuals employed in seven comparable factories. The total scores of these individuals were significantly correlated ($r = +0·78$) with their total responses to six other statements, also scattered at random throughout the forty-one item questionnaire, suggesting job satisfaction. The topics reflected in these six statements were pay and incentives, supplies and services, and work planning. Thus the "group-integration" topics of Figure 4 reflect those of job satisfaction: the opportunity to learn is a reward in itself.

Further analysis of these results showed a strong factory effect over and above the individual effect. In other words, there were highly significant differences between the mean perceptions of the seven samples of factory workers. In some samples the scores on the four system-beta items were positive throughout, in others negative. These factory means were also correlated with the means of the six responses to statements indicating satisfaction with employment. A similar result is described on page 124, not among shop floor workers commenting on their relations with their foremen, but among graduate managers commenting on the administration of which they themselves are the elements. The same effect has been found among a sample of about a hundred foremen in the same chemical plant, employing nearly twenty thousand workers.

The Nature of Advice

A manager is not always able, for a variety of reasons, to work through every step of system beta by himself or with his own staff. He seeks the advice of a friend or of an industrial consultant. He contrives, in other words, to reconnoiter his problem from above. The nature of this expedition generally follows system beta.

1. *Survey Stage.* A man does not seek advice until he is aware and convinced that he needs advice. Nothing is more exasperating than gratuitous advice of which one believes oneself to have no need. One's admission of a need for advice can come only after one has, by a thorough survey of the field, become aware that unaided one can find no easy way out of an undesired situation.

2. *Decision Stage.* If the person seeking the advice cannot himself suggest a promising course of action, at least it remains for

5

him to select the adviser. The need for this decision is still there and one man will choose as his adviser only another person with whom he can identify himself in the problem situation, or, in simple English, only another man in whom he has confidence. This may also be described as a stage of analogy, for the perception of the problem suggests a matching with a particular adviser (see p. 116).

3. *Action Stage.* A man considering the advice of another, even of a close friend with whom he has a deep identification, is likely to prefer advice suggesting action that he himself can take, rather than resign responsibility for the execution of the action as well as for its design. Thus, in selecting from the advice available to him the manager is, in his mind, working through the plan offered, judging its practicability at every step, estimating the cost of following it as it is specified, envisioning economies, halting at anticipated snags, putting questions back to his adviser, making constructive additions, suggesting alternative courses, even at times finishing with a plan better than either his adviser or himself would be capable of thinking up unaided.

4. *Inspection Stage.* The literary critic not infrequently makes his living by ridiculing books that he could not write himself; and the man who seeks external advice is generally more disposed to evaluate severely the outcome of it than he would be to inquire critically into the consequences of his own plan. When one cannot explore the jungle by finding one's own way through it, one is also reluctant to accept the forecasts of another as to where his path will lead.

5. *Control Stage.* Once the inspection stage has been passed, whether in reality or only in the imagination, the consolidating action is generally soon taken. If the advice is seen to work the adviser will probably be invited to tackle fresh problems; if the advice is thought to be indifferent or ineffective, then it will be rejected and the adviser, perhaps, with it. Not seldom, the adviser, on the other hand, by pursuing the reasons for his advice to be rejected, takes his client once more through the system beta cycle, to the benefit of both.

The system beta cycle as it applies to advice can, thus, be summarized

1. Survey: recognition of need and of own inability
2. Decision: identification with decision-agent or adviser
3. Action: criticism of operational proposals of adviser
4. Inspection: skepticism about outcome of advice
5. Control: acceptance or rejection of advice and promotion or dismissal of adviser

It may be helpful at this point to represent the two decision processes (on one's own initiative or at the suggestion of an adviser) as variations on the system beta model, together with the scientific method and the learning process to be further developed shortly (see p. 105). Such a representation is Figure 5. The paradigm is precisely that of Figure 3, in terms of business functions, and of Figure 4, in terms of leadership behavior.

Social and Emotional Aspects

The next pages are devoted to relating the system beta paradigm to the behavior of particular managers, as the individuals they happen to be, introducing into the decision process their own personal biases and perceptions. In jargon, these are some of the unavoidable noises in the circuit, making less detectable the structure of the desirable strategy. However, apart from tracing the idiosyncracies of particular individuals as sources of disturbance, the policy maker has also the social task of translating system beta into managerial action. At all stages he needs to work constructively with other people; whether collecting information to identify the elements of system alpha (stage beta one); integrating what he discovers with the potential interests of other managers to design a first feasible strategy (stage beta two); or at any other of the critical steps in Figure 2, he must be identifying, using or even generating the commitment of colleagues. He needs their support, not only when collecting information and forming plans, but even more so when action must be taken; he needs not only estimates of expenditure but

outside event
↓
first state → new idea → trial action → field check → second state

conjectural creativity

experiential evaluation

assemble data	propose hypothesis	perform experiment	interpret results	evaluate hypothesis
survey problem area	form own trial plan or seek advice	act on own part or appoint agent	inspect or audit outcomes	adopt, modify or reject plan or advice
review old knowledge	infer new knowledge	try out in practice	observe consequences	remember or forget

FIGURE 5 — Showing scientific method, management decision and learning process as aspects of system beta paradigm.

The top row suggests (a) the impact of an event upon a first condition; (b) the emergence of a new idea in consequence; (c) the action taken on this new idea; (d) the check-up on the results of this action; and (e) the second condition attained through the experience as a whole.

Conjectural creativity (feedforward) is the projection into the future of the possible effects of employing the new idea: "How do we use it? What is it likely to do?" Experiental evaluation (feedback) is the comparison of outcome with expectation, both in imagination and in practice.

The second row shows the logical sequence of the scientific method. Any single step of this may involve a system beta analysis of its own before it is admitted to the overall cycle shown; for example, the assembly of the data may involve judging the value of previous experiments in this area, and this evaluation itself may demand a system beta approach.

The third row, divided, shows the structure of a management decision, either taken on one's own part or with the help of advice and an agent. The cycle shows how the appointment of an agent may demand from the principal a clear view of his plan and of the criteria by which its success is to be judged.

The fourth row shows the part played by system beta within the learning process of system gamma (see above 5).

also promises of funds, forecasts and allocations of manufacturing capacity, schedules of availability of the means of distribution, and he needs them at different times and perhaps with different measures of urgency. Sometimes his support needs to come from one key person alone, sometimes from a temporary coalition, sometimes from an established department. During these negotiations he will need a good amount of such notions as incentive, motivation, and group interests, as the relative importances of different issues at different times to different persons, and as the need to treat them as local, temporary, and specific. There may well be general principles of negotiation, as these paragraphs try to make out, but their *emergence is always uniquely situational.* The ability to read the singular details of each situation in terms of the systems alpha and beta, proper both to himself and those around him, is one that, over and above his personal gifts, the industrial negotiator can set out to acquire. Within the broad lines of the program he constructs around Figure 3, his personal approach to others should reflect that suggested in Figure 4. The action phases of our score of projects form, in one sense, a sample of structured searches; as their results become apparent it may be possible to identify more clearly the conditions for successful action, that is, for the effective interplay of systems alpha and beta.

Aspects of Learning: System Gamma

The sets of questions so far suggested to identify the three stages of system alpha and the cycle to identify the five of system beta are, it might be supposed, asked here by an abstracttion. So far the tasks of decision design and decision negotiation have been treated with an impersonal and academic detachment. However, in real life an individual must pose these questions, and it must be asked how he, as the singular being he is, interacts with the two systems and affects their joint output.

It has been observed that the logic of system beta is not only that of trial and error as applied to a (so-called) rational decision; it is the logic of the scientific method and of the learning process here assumed (see figure 5). Both the scientist and the student advance their knowledge by speculating, and by testing their speculations against any observable outcomes of that result. On the one hand, there is verification by the experimental method; on the other hand, the reinforcement of an opinion because it works, to a greater or less, but always significant, degree in practice. These are logically identical conditions. Thus the prudent decision maker, following the cycle of system beta, is not only helping to change the actual state of affairs; he is continually checking his own expectation of what will happen against what he observes actually to happen, and he will contrive to build an information system that helps him to do this.

The processes of inspection should thus continuously audit not only the events that take place; they should also audit the patterns of thought in the mind of the manager influencing these events. The manager should perceive that any outcomes that need subsequent review probably do so, not because the forces at work in the situation changed in the meantime, but because he, or his colleagues, had an incorrect or incomplete view of them. Divergences between expectation and experience, when described, therefore supply the manager with information and enable him to learn. However, the extent to which the manager is conscious of a possible need to change the assumptions on which he is working is a highly personal affair (see p. 127). If he refuses to admit the possibility that his perceptions of what is going on do not correspond to reality, there is little hope that any analysis of his ongoing experience by the system beta paradigm will help him. If he has no wish to learn, because he feels he has no need to do so; or if he admits a need, but cannot endure the doubts and the assaults of exchanging one set of beliefs for another; or if he feels that his need to learn is confined to collecting more technical facts rather than to questioning the validity of his existing thought-programs; then, in any of these cases, it is unlikely that his practical experience can be made the ladder to higher levels of managerial effectiveness and to the simple satisfactions of enlarging his vision.

Hence there is a symbiosis in action between the manager and the situation he is trying to manage (see Figure 6). As he observes the effects of his anticipations on the reality he is trying to change, he may find that any of the elements that he introduces into his system alpha design do not give him the result that he expects. He may find that he has wrongly assessed the value systems of the key managers around him, of whom he may be one; he may be misinformed about the opportunities offered by the external system; and he may have used faulty estimates of the capacity of the internal system available to the enterprise. Insofar as he is able to identify the discrepancies between what he first took to be the condition and what operational experience suggests that the condition actually was, and insofar as he is able to change his perception accordingly, it can be said that the manager is learning.[12] Likewise, a manager may learn from his reflections upon the negotiation aspects of his decision. He now asks whether, instead of following sufficiently the cycle of system beta, he is taking dangerous short cuts, such as at the survey stage omitting critical facts and introducing unjustifiable assumptions. It is by focusing attention on these particular points of the system-alpha/system-beta matrix that he will develop a critical frame of reference in which learning becomes possible.

In the chapter specifically devoted to a theory of learning, this symbiosis between the manager and the system he is trying to influence is examined more closely. But we may here anticipate the result of a further survey, among fifty senior managers working together and frequently joined in common discussion: There is a highly significant correlation between the individual's expressed awareness of his own needs to learn, S (self-awareness), and his expressed interest in the needs of those around him, P (people-awareness).

The symbiosis is not now dwelled on merely as the outcome of this survey to determine the attitudinal structure of managerial motivation. It is, in fact, the key to the design of the Inter-University Program. The particular design chosen emerges from the belief that managers, like all other conscious creatures, learn to take effective action only by having taken effective action, and by an awareness of their success in changing the actual management situations into which they are thrust. It is vital to be clear upon this crucial point. A man *may well learn to talk about taking action simply by talking about taking action* (as in classes at a business school) but to learn *to take action* (as some-thing distinct from learning to talk about taking action) then he needs *to take action* (rather than to talk about taking action) and to see the effect, not of talking about taking action (at which he may appear competent) but *of taking the action itself* (at which he may fall somewhat short of competent). In this taking of action, there is an interchange between the manager, as a person, and the situation he manages. This interchange is represented as system gamma, the effect of the change or action upon the manager, in one direction, and its complementary effect upon the situation, in the other.

The Essence of the Inter-University Program

In order to represent system gamma so that progress with it may be made in real situations, we must first represent the ele-ments of system alpha (that is, the model of the desired outcome or of our strategic objectives) by their fixed and modifiable parts. No amount of learning or improvement within a system can in-fluence the objective facts of nature; it is unlikely, for example, that advances in psychology will ever enable men to drive two or more cars simultaneously, much as many might wish to do so. Hence, if as the first element of system alpha the external system is chosen, we may begin to represent it, first, by the facts of the market—that there is such and such a real demand for, say, motor car insurance—and, second, by the means we have of tapping that market, or even of knowing about it. Without being too philosophical, it can be said that there is an objective demand and a subjective estimate of that demand; they differ insofar as the system (largely of communications between differ-ent levels and across different departments) available to the management for (subjectively) assessing the (objective) demand is defective, and thus, perhaps, capable of improvement by some process of institutional development. The Inter-University Program, personified by the fellow, is such a process. Three concepts can be generalized as the *actual problem in field, mana-gerial reporting channels*, and *facts about field-problem* as given to manager; they are so represented in Figure 6.

managerial symbiosis-system gamma

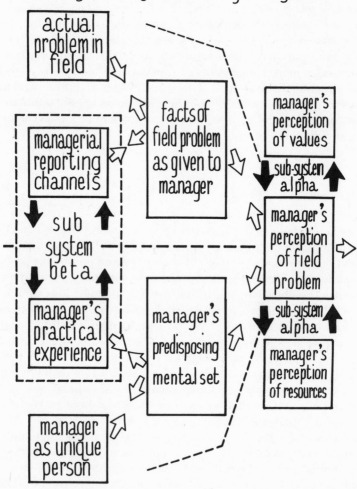

FIGURE 6—Showing integration of sub-system alpha (decision design) and sub-system beta, (decision negotiation) into the learning process of the manager and the change process of the enterprise (system gamma).

Figure 6 may be taken as an expansion of the first entry of the third row of Figure 5, "survey problem area." The manager needs some perception of what

In the same way, the manager (or fellow) dealing with the problem may be represented as a combination of a unique personality[13] overlaid by a fabric of variable experience; these combine to build within his consciousness a set of predisposing mental schemata for processing whatever facts are brought to his attention.[14] These three concepts, too, may be generalized, as in Figure 6, as *manager as unique person, manager's practical experience,* and *manager's predisposing mental set.* Finally, the particular manager's perception of the nature of the particular field problem follows from the interaction between the facts as given to the manager and that manager's predisposing mental set, as suggested in Figure 6. We may repeat the argument for the other two elements of system alpha, namely, managerial values and the internal system. As in his assessment of the field problem, the manager's estimate of the goals of his endeavors and of the resources available to him in the task of reaching these goals are alike strongly colored by his own personal qualities and experience, as well as by the supposed properties of the enterprise itself.

It is thus no pure, impartial, unbiassed assessment of the field problem, of the enterprise goals, nor of the operating resources that the manager enters into his first models of system alpha. His processes of survey or data collection are contaminated from the very start, not only by himself as a unique person and his previous set of unique formative experiences but also by the qualities and distortions of the human organization through which he is trying to collect his data, let alone to achieve his objectives. But by trying to work with these imperfect inputs, through system beta, continually comparing results with forecasts, he may be able to promote the correction and enrichment of his own experience, and also the clarification and reinforce-

---

the field problem may be in order to form his first system alpha design for treating it. Figure 6 shows what may be involved in forming this perception. In particular, the interaction between the individual manager and the system by which he secures information about the field problem is the system beta cycle of Figure 4, and Figure 6 itself is the first step in a system beta cycle of which the second step is the trial decision produced by the sub-system alpha shown. Figure 6 is an example of the continuous repetition of system beta at all stages and sub-stages of system beta itself (see p. 144).

ment of the organizational and the decision-making potential of the management reporting channels. These were two of the program's objectives; the third was to discover whether the staff of the universities could learn anything by helping the managers and the fellows economically to reach them by these paradigms. This symbiosis was the essence of the program and settled the methods of work within each project. Each of the score of these reflects a system gamma, built around the model of Figure 6. Nor is this all. System gamma was the essence, not only of the projects in this particular program, which for all its simplicity, remains a highly factitious and stylized maneuver: system gamma represents in its own way the structure of all intelligent behavior, and offers, in conjunction with systems alpha and beta, one starting point for a general theory of human action, for a science of praxeology. It is also a logical basis of a study of roles; in any situation of achievement, how does one man interact with others? What, in particular, is the contract of each fellow seen in the light of system gamma?

Self-Awareness and People-Awareness

Just as the previous discussions about the use of systems alpha and beta in the practical occasions of management listed some of the operational questions essential to decision making, so must the key questions posed by the use of system gamma be identified. The manager may start with his own self-awareness (see p. 127; subset S) as he addresses himself to the problem on which he has to form or recommend a policy.

He might ask himself:

What kind of a person do I believe myself to be? How far are others likely to share my opinion of myself? What kind of a career have I had, and to what extent is it the career that I expected? How far has my life turned out to be different from anything I might have planned for it? For example, what use do I make of my professional education? And how many times, if at all, and for what reasons, have I ever changed my profession completely? Or have I always kept close to the line

I started out on? Am I, in other words, still the kind of businessman I was at the start? If so, is this because I was right the first time, and never needed to change? Or am I unwilling to take risks, so that I always stick to familiar patterns of thought and activity? If I have specialized, is this because I have become expert, or simply because I prefer the routines I know? Apart from my professional accomplishments, what kind of personality structure have I got, and how does it color my approach to management? Am I, for example, hostile to authority, or indifferent to it, or even submissive? Am I insecure? Or am I so secure, so confident that things will turn out well in the end, that I take quite improvident risks? What kind of defense mechanisms do I invoke when I seem not to be very sure of myself?[15]

In the same way each manager should have occasion to reflect upon his relations to people in general (see Figure 4 and also p. 127, subset P); and such questions as these would be relevant:

What impact do I make on other people? How clear do I make myself to them?[16] Do I listen to what they are trying to say to me? (And do I continue to listen if I discover that those who are trying to tell me something about their own problems are really quite unimportant persons, insofar that nothing they can let me know could ever be of the least benefit to me?) When I find myself talking to others, what is the balance of question and answer? Do I put most of the questions? Do others ask me things? If I do not know the answer, do I say so? Do others ever say that they are not sure what questions they want to put to me, and then ask my help in framing them? Do others often take the initiative to raise with me complex problems that soon reveal how much both of us have to learn? After such a discussion, do the others ever return afterwards with quite different problems, to argue out in the same way? Does it often happen that a superior totally rejects a proposal or report of mine on first meeting it, but changes his mind and becomes positive after a few days? Would it occur to me to ask what had happened? Would I see this as a lesson for myself as well as or even more than for my superior?

Relation to Decision Design (System Alpha)

The discussion of the learning process set into motion by confronting the manager with a real situation has so far been confined to the factors of self-awareness, S, and of awareness of others, P. It is necessary also to touch upon the incidence of the external events that every manager necessarily deals with in his substantive task.

For this discussion, the visiting fellow of the Inter-University Program is treated as if he were a home manager. Although he is not on the paid staff of his host enterprise, and although he has opportunity only to recommend and not to execute, he is, in this last respect, no different from any permanent members of the enterprise who, it is to be supposed, devote some of their time and energy to bringing about change within it. For they too have powers only to advise, and recommend; insofar as action is to be initiated this will largely rest with those to whom they too offer their advice. In practice, once the management of the host enterprise had accepted their visiting fellow's argument in principle, they generally asked at once for him to set up and motivate some task force to make it effective. A vision of possible success in action often made them very impatient. Thus, the relations of the visiting fellow to the decision process can be represented by the same system gamma model as we use to represent the equivalent relations of a manager at home within his organization.

This is shown, slightly rearranged, for one fellow and for one home manager only, in Figure 7 (p. 108); the rearrangement is to make clear that, although the fellow, F, and manager, M, are different human beings, with different personalities, P_F and P_M, different overlays of education and experience, E_F and E_M, securing their date, D_F and D_M, about the external world, R, through different channels, C_F and C_M, it is, nevertheless, at any particular moment of any particular conversation, the same external world that interests them both. It is assumed in this that, however distracted either may be by other events, at the time of the local manager and the fellow meeting to discuss some aspect of the project, they do succeed in directing their individual attentions significantly to the particular business in hand. Their differences of personality structure and of past experience will endow each with different mental sets, S_F and S_M. These together with their different information channels will lead them to different interpretations, I_F and I_M, of what that external world, R, may be. But the assumption underlying each project is that both are making an honest effort to grasp better this underlying and objective reality.

If this is not so,[17] the argument is invalid and the program is misconceived. No doubt, different interpretations can be put upon the conveniently obscure phrase "to grasp better this underlying and objective reality," but, having to stand on his feet before a group of other fellows, or before a group of other managers already involved in a project elsewhere, and to say a few words about his progress, a fellow would soon find himself embarrassed by the comments and questions of his discriminating audience should he fail to convey to them an impression of realistically delving into the structure of some external system.

It can be supposed that Manager M has, in trying to control Reality R, formed of it his impression, I_M. He compares this with the impression, I_F, formed by Fellow F. This opportunity for both to learn is shown in Figure 7 (p. 108) as L_{FM}. Operationally, this may mean that the manager reads a detailed report by the fellow about R; it may merely mean that during an interview between manager and fellow something is said that reveals, perhaps like a flash of midnight lightning, a difference of interpretation that leads to further questions. However this may be, the comparisons and contrasts of I_F and I_M may soon lead back, either to R or to the more personal elements of E and P. If I_F and I_M differ significantly, then either the data on which each is postulated differ, or the same data are differently processed by the two different sets of mental resources, or both sets of factors differ throughout. If it is that the two sets of data differ, then a discussion about where they come from may be helpful; the two sets of communication channels may be compared and some instructive lessons may be learned. Where, for example, R stands for the morale of the subordinate staff and C_F has been opened up by the fellow using sociological survey techniques not previously known to the management, the interaction between I_F and I_M may be profound; examples are common.[18] On the other hand, in the early stages of a project, I_F may be comparatively defective because the fellow has not had access to sufficient data; and this may be because parts of C_F are held closed before him. Either way, specific measures to open up the channels of communciation can soon be suggested.

However, I_F and I_M may differ, not because the samples of data on which they are based can be shown to differ, but because the two mental sets, S_F and S_M, can be understood to differ. One obvious reason for this difference may be traced to differences between E_F and E_M; the fellow may be an expert in accounting, or in production planning, or in marketing, whereas the manager is a generalist not very well versed in, say, the inventory puzzles of direct costing, or heuristic sequencing models, or the determination of pricing policy. Equally, the fellow may be off his own ground, talking to a manager who is accomplished in the affairs under review. Yet even in such conditions, provided that the discussion is reasonably well structured, the inexpert novice may yet put questions to the acknowledged authority enabling him to use even more effectively the expert power that he commands. As far as it was possible to do so in the time at their disposal, all fellows were given enough practice in the art of interviewing to encourage such outcomes.

Differences between I_F and I_M may, on the other hand, spring from differences between P_F and P_M. If the manager is highly authoritarian, for example, whereas the fellow believes that the subordinate's views in any situation are worth hearing, it might well be that although the manager and the fellow were in complete agreement about the facts of R—that, say, the workmen were deliberately restricting their output and hence their earnings, according to some formula agreed among themselves in secret—the manager refused to entertain any interpretation of these facts other than could be provided, say, by Theory X. His adhesion to this theory might not have followed from any careful analysis of human behavior; it might be a simple reflection of his own early experiences of life, under an authoritarian parent. This is hardly a topic likely to be pursued in depth as part of the program itself, which does not pretend to undertake psychotherapeutic treatment. At the same time, it is already clear that some enterprises are taking to heart the emotional and temperamental features of management behavior, and fellows have been more than a little surprised by the readiness with which, given a structured approach to the subject, powerful top managers are willing to discuss before each other their own prejudices and shortcomings, as these have been revealed in the course of the projects (see also p. 126, dealing with managerial self-development).

Internal Resources

Figure 7 shows a small element from a representation that can be indefinitely replicated. It is a comparison between the interpretations made by two different persons at the first stage of system beta (survey) of one of the three elements of system alpha (externals). It would be unrealistic to suggest that much learning would accrue because two men happened to draw different conclusions (I_F and I_M) merely from once surveying the same local and transitory externals. Managers inhabit a fast-moving world and often find themselves in conflict with other managers; they have little time to spend over every disagreement among themselves about the nature of the world around them, or to trace its effects upon the total management situation. However, when Figure 7 is drawn twice again, once to enter on the left-hand box the strength of the internal resources of the enterprise rather than the opportunities of its external world, and a second time to enter the value system of those in effective control, the possibility of instructive discussion becomes somewhat more vivid.

The systemic approach, using alpha, beta, and gamma alike, may become habitual. Although the attitude of busy managers toward the outside world may well be one of *ad hoc* trial and error—finding out about the market empirically by trying to sell in it rather than analytically by comparing the independent surveys of responsible agents—it is less likely that they would

6

take the same unstructured or even random attitude toward determining the potential and the usage of their own internal resources. Experience seems to suggest that such independent estimates are rarely made: the occasions for making them do not seem readily to occur and they are seldom contrived.[19] Such elementary guides as management ratios and exercises in cost-benefit analysis, seldom point out the future. Although most management information systems give regular, detailed, and accurate estimates of the current usage of particular and local physical resources, including cash, it seems rare for the top management of a firm to work its way through a call-over of the internal system, such as is suggested on p. 35, system alpha. The allocation and use of critical resources will generally reward inspection. At this juncture, however, even more than such a call-over is asked here: it is being asked that it be done against the framework of system gamma, Figure 7, by those who command the levers of strategy.

A realistic appreciation of the internal resources of an enterprise demands that the interpretations thereof made by different judges – whether managers helped by a fellow, or managers on their own – should be contrasted and crosschecked against not only what the different communication channels make available to the different individuals, but also against the different mental sets by which they interpret the data at their disposal. Perhaps the most precious resource of those in charge of European industry is the talent and the potential motivation of its middle management, which could, in turn, awaken the energies of its subordinate supervisors. Yet, again and again, the independent studies of the visiting fellows revealed how little of this enormous fund is brought into effective action. To some extent, the model of Figure 7 is helpful in analyzing this frustrating state of affairs. If the interpretation, I_M, made by a given top manager of his human resources differs from that made by another top manager, or from that, I_F, made by the visiting fellow, it may be for two main reasons, both of which can clearly be traced in Figure 7. It may be that the clarity – or opacity – of the two communication channels, C_F and C_M, differs significantly. The fact that the fellows were not colleagues permanently in the same organization may mean that they were spoken to more frequently and more openly than are the line superiors above the middle management; on the other hand, there may have been resistance to the questions of some unattached outsider, however seductively posed. Only the actual situation can suggest the explanation for any difference of transparency that might be found; the field observations of the fellows, supporting flow models and action sequences, are rich with suggestions, and it is interesting to note how often these men were struck, on their American tour, by the comparative openness of the lines of command which they were able to trace at first hand in the giant corporations they visited.

Figure 7 suggests that local resource interpretation may be defective for other and more personal, reasons. The mental sets, S_M, of top managers themselves may, however unconsciously, introduce into the final interpretation, I_M, elements not suggested by the data. Some top managers, for example, may be insecure enough to fear that their subordinates are continually watching for chances to pass upward inaccurate or incomplete information, which may lead, in the end, to the subordinates telling their superiors just what they think the superiors would like to hear, whether it is true or not. There is, in other words, an interaction between P_M and C_M. Or it may be a top manager's previous experience, E_M, that introduces bias into his mental set and distorts his interpretation of what his subordinates are trying to say.

Managerial Values

A corporate strategy demands (system alpha) a view of the external world, of the internal resources and of the managerial values of the enterprise. It was the experience of the majority of the fellows that, in their host enterprises as a group, the formation of long term plans was more frequently hindered by inadequate definitions of value systems than by information about prospects and means, imperfect though these could also be, and often were. It was for the fellows themselves to give examples, particularly in contrasting European and American experience. However, three general points can be made. First, although technologies exist for searching, and terminologies for describing, both externals and internals, on the whole there is a lack of any nomenclature for objectively classifying the fields of human values. Some content of these fields has already been suggested in the discussions of system alpha (p. 34), but in the absence of objective measuring scales, there is in practice no satisfactory alternative to members of the top management meeting face-to-face, preferably in the presence of a disinterested outsider, to thrash out such questions as "What, if anything, do we really believe in? Rather let us discuss what, beneath our coalitions and our compromises, we would honestly like to do. Let none of us say what we do not mean; that is all we need to promise." These possibilities of self-revealment may surprise those who encounter them for the first time, but there is evidence enough, from the projects themselves, that in some enterprises they do not lie too deeply concealed to resist reasonable efforts to bring them to the surface. Such then, is the first point: the surprising rarity of open discussion of the value systems of the top management, collective as well as personal.

The second is the unconscious assumption that a general and indefatigable wish to make money and to be efficient is an adequate expression of final goals. The fact that this may be a necessary condition does not, however, also make it sufficient. Nevertheless, a situational review of system alpha, involving once more the disinterested outsider, may soon identify the list of questions needed to contain the policy of profit and efficiency inside a realistic and operational frame. Such then is the second point: the common belief that a determination to be profitable is a practically sufficient lodestone for success. The third conclusion of the projects is that an absence of values, whether forever concealed or whether openly advertised by unsettling shifts of policy, is sensitively reflected at all levels of the organization; where those in charge do not know by what marks they are trying to navigate, they cannot delegate responsibility to their officers and these cannot issue consistent orders to their men. Granted that strategies can be determined .

only after the external and the internal objectivities are known, but the clearer the knowledge of these the more imperative any lack of definition of the more subjective value system.[20]

NOTES

1. As the program developed it became evident that the organization of the enterprise, namely, the allocation of tasks under system alpha, is also potentially the theme of a further subsystem.
2. The Polish Academy of Sciences has a praxeology section.
3. "For if a man think himself to be something when he is nothing, he deceiveth himself. Let therefore every man prove his own work and then shall he have rejoicing in himself alone, and not in another." (Galatians, Chap. 6, V 3, 4).
4. For a critical discussion of the origins and limitations of traditional organizational theory see Paul Lawrence and Jay Lorsch, *Organization and Environment*. Harvard University Press, 1967.
5. Insofar as his information is not complete, he must take risks; so long as he feels able to bear these risks, his information remains adequate.
6. The use of the expression "value system" is a most convenient way of conveying what is, in reality, a complex set of ideas. It is an observable fact that a man interacts with the society around him; this interaction includes, on the part of both the man and society, not only an awareness of the present, but a reflection of the past and an anticipation of the future. Societies have not only immediate desires and published policies that act as their guardians of the moment, but customs, traditions, and formal laws that embody their past experience, or at least the experience of those in power. Thus the memory, awareness, and anticipation of the individual are matched against the corresponding qualities of the society. What the man wants to do is governed by his past and his future as much as by his present, and what society will allow him to do is similarly structured. To know how far he can go before what the manager wants to do conflicts with what society will permit him to do is, in one sense, a mark of the innovator. The car, when it first appeared, had to be preceded by a man on foot waving a red flag, because it otherwise offended the existing law. In Wales the entrepreneur who wishes to sell beer on Sunday would even today find his value system in conflict with that of local society.
7. In Figure 1 all the entries are grossly oversimplified. The primitive savage not only wishes, in planning the jungle expedition, to satisfy his hunger. His value system may embrace a score of other elements — to kill his quarry for its skin or its feathers; to train his son in stalking or in archery; to bring home food for others, not only to satisfy hunger but to celebrate a victory over tribal enemies; to try out a new bow; to make peace with a neighbor by cooperating with him in a dangerous enterprise; to reconnoiter some new territory; to provoke war by hunting in the preserves of a neighboring tribe; to return uninjured by lurking beasts; to conserve his supply of arrows. It is important, when many persons, such as a board of directors, are concerned with system alpha, that there is some recognition among them of their diversity of values. Not all individuals would allot the same priorities to the same items, and from time to time the group may need to remind them-

selves about their diverse objectives. There are, of course, the same ranges within the other columns of Figure 1, although the objective study of resources and markets can usually settle which are the critical elements; agreement among the different individuals joining in the decision then secures itself.

8. The outcome of treating the information made available by the continuous processes of survey and trial depends, of course, upon the skill and creativity of the strategist. Skill may be acquired by exercising teachable techniques, such as are developed by operations research and used by the more reputable management consultants. Creativity is harder to command, but among intelligent and experienced men is often inhibited by either a conscious loyalty to traditional practices or an unconscious assumption of unnecessary bounds. (cf. David and Goliath, footnote 3 p. 25). It should be one purpose of the questions set out in the discussion of system alpha to examine how valid are these traditions and how restrictive these assumptions. Creativity may be called the exercise of imagination, if one merely seeks different words for expressing the same ignorance, but imagination is the quality of analogizing, or of seeing that two propositions (or more) are related.

9. The Duchess (of Kent) felt convinced that it was her supreme duty in life to make quite sure that her daughter should grow up into a Christian queen. To this task she bent all her energies; and as the child developed, she flattered herself that her efforts were not unsuccessful. When the Princess was eleven, she desired the Bishops of London and Lincoln to submit her daughter to an examination and report on the progress that had been made. "I find the time to be now come," the Duchess explained in a letter obviously drawn up by her own hand, "that what has been done should be put to some test, that if anything has been done in error of judgment it may be corrected, and that the plan for the future should be open to consideration and revision". Lytton Strachey, *Queen Victoria* (1921), p. 25.

10. In the fourth step of the foregoing process, for example, the check sample has been compared with the first sample to test whether the relationship is uniformly present throughout the universe. The first stage in the new system beta is a survey of the available data—the numbers in the two samples and the distribution of whatever variates we are interested in across the two samples. The second stage is to form a hypothesis about these two distributions, probably a null hypothesis, suggesting that the means and variances in the two samples are not significantly different. The third stage is to perform an experiment, that is, a set of calculations, to determine just what these two differences in fact turn out to be. The fourth stage is to inspect the result of this experiment and to see if it is consonant with the null hypothesis. This is done by referring to statistical tables, to test the significances of the variance ratios and of the difference between the means. The fifth stage is to consider the outcome of these tests and either to accept or reject the null hypothesis. (It may be necessary to draw a third or further sample.)

11. M. I. Hussein, unpublished Ph.D thesis, University of Manchester, 1963.

12. I am indebted to a correspondence with Dr. M. P. Demetrescu of Bucharest for the application of entropy measures to structure these discrepancies.

13. According to A. S. Tannenbaum, "Several aspects of personality are especially pertinent to man's behavior in organizations. First, personality is relatively stable. It is formed during the early years of growth—infancy and

childhood. Once formed, however, the adult personality does not change readily. The individual, therefore, comes to the organization with his personality pretty much as a given. Second, personality characteristics are said to be general. This means simply that an individual tries to express his distinctive personality in a variety of situations. He does not leave his personality at the gate when he enters an organizational role. Third, personality is motivational; it implies strivings, wants, need, or determining tendencies. Characteristics of personality are not simply a way of classifying or typing people, but, more dynamically, they tell us something about what the individual is characteristically trying to do, consciously or unconsciously."

14. This ingenuously simple model of the manager merely says in diagrammatic form that some things about a man may readily be changed by common experience and that others may not. The words significant to this argument are, of course, readily and common; a man may readily learn to read a railway timetable by commonly using it: he may not readily learn to read the minds of other persons by commonly conversing with them. He may learn to do so slowly, by conducting conversations with them of a special character. But at a yet deeper level there are some things that, from ordinary experience, he may never learn; or, in other words, there are some aspects of his being that, without intensive effort of a strikingly unusual nature, he is unlikely to change. Such are his basic personality traits—his defense mechanisms, his attitudes to authority, his sense of security. Although narcotic drugs, deep psychotherapy, major disasters involving the family and other avalanches of adversity may change any or all of us at the centers of our very selves, we take it as an observable fact that a man may readily be changed in some particulars without being changed in others. Thus, the latent patterns of response accessible to the manager are regarded as dependent upon a fixed and a variable set of his qualities. In David Copperfield, Dickens described an amiable character who responded to every suggestion, every new experience, and every natural event with an anecdote about King Charles' head; any variable element in his response was much reduced by his ease of mental access to this fixed and curious image.

15. To this catechism, one fellow added toward the end of the course, "What is an honest man, and what should I do to become one?"

16. "For if the trumpet give an uncertain sound, who shall prepare himself to the battle? So likewise ye, lest ye utter by the tongue words easy to be understood, how shall it be known what is spoken? For ye shall speak into the air. There are, it may be, so many kinds of voices in the world, and none of them is without significance. But if I know not the meaning of the voice, I shall be unto him that speaketh a barbarian and he that speaketh shall be a barbarian unto me" (I Cor. 14:8-11).

17. There are reasons why, at the outset, this might not be so. Some fellows may be more concerned with impressing their hosts with how qualified they are in some particular professional technique, rather than with addressing themselves to the treacherous complexities of some multidimensional reality. While in the early course of establishing himself before strangers, it may be tactically wise to demonstrate expertise in some managerial function, a reasonably secure fellow would soon wish to concentrate on the substantive project. Or the fellow might be too eager to read into the external world a recollection of his past success in a totally different situation, so ignoring relevant features of the present and substituting for them impressions from

elsewhere. The fantasy may, on the other hand, be with the manager rather than with the fellow. Faced with the immediate prospect of searching self-analysis, a manager may try to head off the fellow, to represent the facts as he knows them as even more different from reality than they may already appear to him; or the manager may give the impression of being highly open and cooperative, but, in his heart, hold no intention of acting upon whatever recommendations may emerge from the exercise. It would be interesting to set the fellows a competition, to discover who could produce the longest catalogue of such evasion. On the other hand, an honest but exaggerated enthusiasm to bring about change without a thorough study of the relevant factors might be just as uninstructive and profitless, judged by the overall criteria of the program. All these difficulties multiply the opportunities to learn. Hopefully it will be possible to learn a little about management education and action research in general, and about the Inter-University Program in particular.

18. During a research project that led up to this program, a small group of managers interviewing several hundred managers in other Belgium firms, found that among the fifty topics most frequently raised by those interviewed, the opinion of the population was most negative about unsettling interruptions from above to their daily work. Despite the striking unanimity and pervasiveness of this opinion, it proved extremely difficult for the senior managements seen as responsible to believe the evidence. Only a minority of these then set out to correct what was so widely complained of.

19. It is fairly clear that the projects set up under this program have been, for some enterprises, the first occasion for such reviews at the level of policy formation. More than one enterprise had no reliable costing system, and one had none at all.

20. A lengthy analysis of the reflections made by the fellows on their American experience reveals the following syndrome of discrimination between management cultures on the two sides of the Atlantic:

- Recognition of markets as the main seat of opportunity (system alpha, externals)
- Quantitative assessments of market opportunity supported by adequate data processing (survey stage, system beta)
- Hierarchy of policies built on such assessment (decision stage, system beta)
- Specification of individual tasks inside hierarchy of policies, or management by objectives (action stage, system beta)
- Rigorous control of results by open discussion between different management levels (audit stage, system beta)
- Unhesitating innovation should existing results prove significantly ineffective (control stage, system beta)

Effective management, by the use of information, the setting of policies, the working out of them through hierarchies of objectives and through rigorous control of results has in itself, become a management value. Management, like medicine or the law, has become an activity valued in its own right and not merely as a gainful occupation (system alpha, values).

3

Managerial Action
and Organizational Change

RELATION TO DECISION NEGOTIATION (SYSTEM BETA)

It is by now assumed that the first search for an elaboration of a satisfactory design through system alpha has provisionally opened up the appropriate fields of survey (namely, of values, of externals, and of internals), and that discussions involving different persons to check the *a priori* validity of the first design have already suggested the details both of the action to be taken and of the criteria for judging its effectiveness. But the system beta cycle of negotiation to be met in pursuing a strategy will demand considerably more from its managers than these dialectical exchanges adequate for debating its feasibility during the early design stages. The proposed design must additionally be subjected to a series of systemic examinations across the five stages of system beta, aimed at coloring and strengthening the plan with local detail. Because thereafter it will have passed every inspection or audit save the final test of action in the real world, it may rightly be supposed that there is confidence enough in the chosen design for this test now to be worth making.[1]

71

The negotiation to secure confidence in such action will need to start with a fresh view of the design in terms of system gamma, personal, local, specific, and up to date. It may be helpful, but not enough, that once conducted, a system gamma exercise changes the perceptions of what any of the three decision elements of a situation may be. The actual situations to be managed are also known to change. Some strategic plans have had a checkered history; having once been prepared with great energy and then postponed with equal unanimity, they may be taken from their pigeon holes from time to time, dusted, initialled and put back again. It is always a good idea, when on the brink of action, to confirm, first, whether the particular plan pulled out is the correct one, and second, whether it is still up to date.

It is suggested here that the structure of the checks is to trace the first system alpha design through the system beta cycle of negotiation, employing a recurrent dialogue among managers *aware of the self-questioning processes of system gamma.* In an educational program such as this, the participants should be obliged from time to time to admit openly any changes in their perception of a given strategy, so that they may discuss with others what they think themselves to be learning. To understand that one's view has changed because, under system gamma, one has recognized the inadequacy of a former view is the essence of learning. When the subject about which the view is held can further be located either as an element of system alpha—such as contradictory values or wrongly assumed opportunities—or as an element of system beta—such as inadequate data or insufficient inspection—then learning is assured at the level of theory and of practice alike. But confrontation with reality in the presence of colleagues alone can secure this. It is obvious to all that action alone can change reality; it is by no means obvious that only when reality is so changed can the agent of change himself be changed.

A preliminary survey is thus needed to identify the key activities essential to any operational moves by the enterprise, not only to those flowing from the particular policy in hand. An enterprise should continuously reassure itself about the nature of its critical problems, its crucial resources and the value systems of its key managers. This survey and identification of the governing factors must be rigorously situational from start to finish, and (as the fellows will confirm) any transfer of past experience, however successful at the time, from other sets of conditions should be avoided, or, if unavoidable, treated with the most extreme caution.[2] It may be particularly helpful at this stage to bring into the review any members of the staff known to be opposed to the policy in hand. Typical questions in this *reality-oriented* survey are

What is the true nature of the demand we face, now or in the future? How has it grown from our past activities? Who are the ultimate consumers? Is this demand critically sensitive to certain issues, such as the level of some other market, unrest abroad, domestic fashion, government expenditure, the general state of the economy or even such fantasies as putting men on the moon? In any analysis of what is now going on, what are the critical factors? Where, within the enterprise, does the motivation come from and what reward does it attract? Are we compensating the right people for the right reasons? Are financial margins, raw material supplies, information services, or manufacturing capacities now entirely adequate? What information have we about them? When were the facts last checked? Who did so? What conclusions did he reach? What, if anything, was done about them?

What is likely to happen to these critical factors in the future? What are the risks of manufacturing obsolescence or of shortage of professional skills, of losing key men, or of being overtaken by technical change elsewhere? What of the viability of our distribution channels or sources of supply? Is our research policy adequate? How do we keep enough of our staff in the picture when we wish to bring about changes?

What would we like to govern our pricing policies? Our design policies? Our product policies? What actually governs them in our present situation? What are the significant differences between these ideal and these actual factors?

How will these differences affect us as we set about implementing our plans?

A critical review, in the style of system gamma, of the entire field of information drawn upon for making the first system alpha design should be the responsibility of some individual or group of individuals; it must be followed by a similar review of the resources at the disposal of the decision makers. Survey and provisional policy design should then be followed by a critical review of whatever action, based on available resources, is to implement the plan; and then by a detailed evaluation of the local processes of audit and inspection supposed to monitor the proposed action. It may not tax the ingenuity much to prepare such a catalogue of inquiry as this; it is easy to outline the tasks of others. However, it is more difficult to ensure its application to practice.

THE INNOVATION PARADOX

There is a particular difficulty in the implementation of new policies that deserves special attention in every review. As soon as the key activities upon which the success of the decision depends have been identified, then special resources may need to be brought to support them. If one critical need should be for fresh engineering design then concentrated help may be demanded by the design office in order to specify the new process or device. If the critical question is of distribution, then the sales, transport, and advertising managers may need extra resources (perhaps to be deflected from other managers) to implement some solution to the difficulty. If the question is more general, such as the desirability of a merger, then it may be the entire board of the enterprise that needs help, and help of an unaccustomed kind. It is important for policy makers to ensure that these key needs, local, situational, and specific to the decision in hand, are accurately identified and that adequate support is given to those individuals called upon to handle them. It seems unnecessary to suggest that it is the weakest link in the chain that calls for particular attention. But there is a paradox in such concentration of support: *Any new or specialist solution found by the departmental management nominated to deal with the key problem has to be integrated back into the total system of the enterprise.*[3]

The paradox has long been familiar to surgeons; having successfully treated or even replaced a particular organ, they have had the misfortune to see their patient die because the new equilibrium with the rest of the body demanded by the transplant is not achieved. In management, the new engineering design must be implemented in the existing workshops. The purchasing officer may therefore need to change his supplier as well as his specifications; the stores may need not only to find room for the new parts but also to carry old spares for servicing past and present models; agents providing after-sales service may demand new maintenance procedures; even customers may need particular advice about the change of design, and billing departments may have to keep fresh sets of records. A critical question in the negotiation of a strategic decision is always, therefore, "How do we face simultaneously the opposed issues of new specialization and of traditional integration?" For the integrating function creates ambiguous status relationships, with the official integrator often assuming himself to be the superior and seeing the creative or specialist innovator as his subordinate and not seldom, therefore, as his inferior. These status relationships, rather than any technical or economic constraints, may be the critical determinants of the success or failure of desirable change and should be fully understood by those in power.

Some organizations seem deliberately, or even perversely, designed to preserve a frustrating status quo within its hierarchy or code of precedence. Indeed, it is not unknown in large corporations for individuals unembarrassed by professional qualifications to insinuate themselves into such interceptive roles as "adviser on communication problems," "coordinating director," "interdepartmental representative," "liaison officer," or even "cross-functional controller." If it should become clear to the professional specialists, upon whose technical skill and personal commitment the success of the innovation may depend, that these ostensible integrators may be using their network of contacts principally to consolidate their personal power—and therefore actually to delay or even to prevent change while pretending to promote it—the chances of real change must be remote. Even when such an integrator is also a professionally qualified specialist for whom others have a high personal regard, the problem remains; the subordinate specialists recognize that the integrating task, by needing to assess action priorities, inevitably demands an assessment of their individual performances, and they may on this account withhold from the integrator information seeming to reflect unfavorably upon their part in the cooperative mission as a whole, but nevertheless essential to its success.

The following questions, forming an operational survey, should thus be asked in terms specific to the particular enterprise and to the particular change it is attempting to make:

What precisely are the new tasks to be done? What is special about them? Who is to do them? How and by whom is it expected that they will be reintegrated within our traditional operations?

Does the style of top management encourage such integration or does it actually prevent it? Have the operations of the enterprise been functionally oriented for so long that it has become hard to cooperate even on existing jobs, let alone on new ones? To what extent is the allocation of duties and powers the fruit of genuine negotiation between departments? To what extent is it seen to reflect the authoritarian decisions of the legitimate boss? To what extent is it seen as the log-rolling compromises of uninvolved manipulators? Are the means of allocating tasks to different departments consonant with the demands of the tasks and with the capacities of those in charge of the departments?

Who allocates scarce or critical resources to departments with an overriding need for them? If one critical resource is the time of the top management, who settles the agenda of their discussions? What are the means of preserving any necessary access to such critical resources by departments with (apparently) less imperative claims?

Who is to be alert to the (specialized) opportunities of new technologies in both existing and new markets? Who is to assess the enterprise-wide changes that their possible exploitation will demand? Who is to ensure that coordinating officers do not preserve their jobs by actively inhibiting the very integration they are employed to encourage? How are these officers motivated, by selection, pay, and promotion?

What new problems of integrating specialized tasks will emerge as the enterprise grows? To what extent could the old specialist tasks now be incorporated in those more general? How far can the practice of "job enlargement" be carried as one innovation follows another? Which departments need long-term support for facing changes introduced, by and large, by others?

What kind of information systems, from market intelligence to cost accounting, are in use? In particular, what effective interdepartmental information channels exist? What encouragement is there for operating departments to use them?

What means are there for defining and specifying the interdepartmental tasks to be performed throughout the organization? How far can they be discharged by persons already on the permanent staff of the separate departments involved?

What necessary tasks should the enterprise not be doing at all but contracting to outside firms? What would be the control or inspection problems so created? Are there other economies of scale or work simplification that need constant review?

What are the most common communication and control channels between the centers of decision (policy makers) and peripheries of action (factory, market, laboratory, and office)? How reliable are they? When were they last examined?

This second or *operational* survey, aimed at clarifying the specific action conditions of each specific decision, following upon the first reality-oriented system alpha or design survey, itself aimed at assessing the specific conditions of that decision (values, opportunities, and resources), should put the manager in a commanding position to act upon it. But system beta, the complete cycle of negotiation, demands not only survey, trial decision, and action; it demands audit, recapitulation, and review. What actually follows from the policy decision in reality? The need for such an *inspection* survey suggests at least the following questions:

If divergences appear between what was expected from the policy and what in fact happened, where and what are their probable sources? To what extent were our policies founded upon assumptions that now need to be modified in the light of this experience? If no such modification occurs even after it is evidently called for, why does the enterprise ignore its own experience? Is any lack of follow-up or correction merely departmental, or is it more integrative and organic?

What new searches or studies should any divergences suggest? Has the enterprise unexpectedly encountered (or is it now encountering) trends that might transform its activities radically in the near future? Are the key issues still what were assumed when the management prepared its policies? To what extent do they attribute any success — or lack of it — to the correct causes? In other words, does the original system alpha design still significantly correspond to reality, now that it has been tried out?

Does a successful operation suggest how managers throughout the enterprise might achieve an even better use of their resources? Could they, for example, now open up still further their information flow, clarify more precisely their criteria for judging local effectiveness, simplify their organization, or sharpen more appropriately — not necessarily in pecuniary terms — the incentives to individuals, groups, or departments?

The final stage of system beta — *control or consolidation* within existing experiences or policies — suggests, for any projected or recently implemented decision, such questions as these:

Apart from what the management is hoping to gain from this particular move, so thoroughly planned and evaluated (as, for example, the final decision to enter a new market with a new product made in a new plant, or to merge with an old competitor so as to streamline management, rationalize production, and simplify marketing) what may they also learn about the industry they are in? About its markets, potentials, resources, costs, and so forth? How do the individual members of the top management differently interpret the experiences they have just lived through, in the light of these more general questions? Do these experiences cause any individual members to question such fundamental issues as the self-image of the firm, or perhaps the need to establish one? Has the particular exercise in decision making raised such issues as the firm's reputation for price, quality, delivery intervals, after-sales service, employee relations, growth, technical leadership? Has it shown up weaknesses in the top management structure itself? Or made individual members of it recognize, perhaps for the first time, that on certain aspects of the firm's strategic activities—such as investment policies or search for greater market share—they may be in deep opposition to their colleagues? If so, what is the effect of this likely to be for future growth? How is any potential conflict likely to affect the broader future of the firm?

At the level of top management, such questions as these can, of course, be posed by external consultants, by pure system alpha designers and pure system beta organizers. For them to do so would always be instructive. But the ultimate reward for such probings lies in the personal involvement they demand of the line managers, in exploring their own values and their own goals, their own beliefs and their own dispositions towards risk. Only the free comparison of personal impressions among confiding colleagues, as suggested in the models of system gamma, can engender permanent change in these subjective elements of the decision process. Of all the aspects of policy formation to which the fellows gave their undivided attention for almost a year, it was the value systems of the top management that seemed to them least clearly recognized, least often discussed, and, as a medium of integration, least effectively exploited.

The Problem in Retrospect

The following observations were written after the first program was over. They try to reflect, in terms of the model of social negotiation drawn from the experience of the fellows, the first essential steps in their deliberate efforts to introduce major change. Much has been written on the subject of change, and on the roles of change agents, but what is still lacking is a simple model that might be used by all managers at all times to plan their explorations of the unknowns that lie ahead of them. The problem has two main dimensions, to say the least: first, the social psychiatrists have themselves to identify the structure and dynamics of institutional diagnosis and therapy; second, they have to convey their understanding of these processes to the mass of managers whose daily task it is to direct and control the social and industrial institutions on which our modern-day economy depends. We do not lack evidence to suggest that, in all known cultures—European, American, Russian, Japanese, Asian, and African—this direction and this control still have their moments of disappointment; little is likely to be lost, therefore, if we try to set down our experience, such as it may be, of how a handful of practical managers actually set about trying to introduce a few ideas intended to be helpful to their hosts. The note ends with some practical advice about action firmly in mind; over two centuries ago, Hannah Glasse began a celebrated cookery recipe, "Take your hare when it is cased" (misquoted as "First catch your hare"), and there is today an equal need to attend to the supply of graduates capable of developing into managers of innovation and of strategic growth. I believe that this need will not be met, at least upon a useful scale, until there is agreement upon the social purpose and intellectual mission of our universities. I also believe the views expressed here on this subject are shared by the fellows whose experience has enabled me to formulate them.

PROBLEMS OF ACCESS TO AUTHORITY

The five steps of system beta (survey, trial decision, action, inspection, and control, with feedback from the process of inspection to the decision-maker) are, no doubt, a self-evident sequence. But they hold the key to the processes of institutional change or organizational development, or, more generally, to that complex interplay of individuals by which the management of an enterprise fulfills its latent policies.

Consider the system beta cycle in the round. Even if the visiting fellow, or other author of change, is himself clear about their operational character, the five steps can be expressed, or implemented, only with the approval of the manager in charge of the organization, or of any group therein, where the cycle is to unfold; if this individual is in a subordinate position, this approval may be imposed upon him by a superior, but, if, as in the Inter-University Program, the changes are sought at a strategic level, only the policy-making board of the enterprise, represented perhaps by the president or other chief executive, can give a first approval to the change being attempted. Because the fellow has no formal authority, and he may be attempting a tricky negotiation, it is evident that this approval should be diplomatically sought and then discussed as a learning experience for those in charge of the enterprise.[4] Unless the client, or person in charge of the organization to be changed, is made aware of the stress that the attempt to change it may bring to bear upon him, and that in this attempt he may be obliged to recognize his own need to be changed, it is useless to proceed. The total organization inside which the system beta cycle is to be traced includes the person in charge of it, and, because no part of any organization can be changed without in some degree changing every other, it is essential that this key person enters the experiment with a reasonably open mind. For one important cause for reports upon difficult or delicate situations to be so readily shelved may be found in the threat they offer to the managements responsible for handling them; if independent study reveals that those in charge believe (or wish to believe) the situation to be markedly different from what the impartial evidence suggests, it is unlikely that much effective correction can be launched before that belief has been re-examined by those who hold it. A change in the perception that the management has of its role and powers—that is, a change in its own self-perception—becomes a preliminary essential to success.

Such changes in self-perception are not easy to bring about, although there is a little evidence that groups of top managers who recognize their colleagues from other firms to be in the same boat may help to open each other's eyes. Thus, on the threshold of any attempt to develop new policies or new procedures in an organization, whether based on the inspiration of a visitor from outside or not, lies the problem of managerial self-understanding; access to the secret of innovation is, in fact, access to the value system of those who would introduce it. Indeed, many managers who complain that it is easy for them to understand a situation but impossible to change it need to recognize that it may well be they themselves, embedded at the heart of the situation, who supply the core of the resistance.

Problems of Communication

Given that an attempt at organizational development, such as product innovation or market expansion, has been launched in security enough to ensure the continued support of those in command of the organization, it becomes necessary to examine the problems of internal communication within the organization itself.

The process with which the system beta cycle opens, that of survey, observation, or search, is likely to be much concerned with the working peripheries of the enterprise. What, in fact, goes on at the point of production or at the point of sale, as distinct from what is reported to the boss? What do the workmen and their supervisors actually do, feel, and think? What are the customers' true needs? How does the system of shop floor maintenance or supply really work? What are the inner goals, the personal drives, of the trade union members, as distinct from the various mythologies about them propagated by trade union officials, by line managers, by personnel officers, by professors of industrial relations, and by the experts of government departments concerned with productivity and employment? The questions seem endless, and, even when they have been answered, the task has only begun. For the seeker after truth may then have difficulty in transposing what he has found out into the second phase of the system beta cycle, and for two reasons. First, he may be suspected as the agent of a power structure whose interests are not those of the levels he examines; the evidence that he collects may thus be distorted, incomplete, or even deliberately misleading. Second, the activity characterizing the second phase of system beta, namely, trial decision, is normally conducted at a level higher—and, not seldom, much higher—than that at which the search or fact-finding is aimed. All the problems of access noted in the previous paragraph are thus raised again. Those who have the authority to interpret the working-level situation in terms of trial decisions are often unwilling to accept any evidence collected about that situation; they may even be divided among themselves, and the evidence may be used by one senior management faction against another. They may be united and agree on the evidence, but, instead of building it into their decisions to improve their own organization, they may choose to employ it for attacking some third party.

However this may be, there are often difficult problems in feeding the products of the survey stage, no matter how accurate and authentic, into the stage of trial decision. These may demand hardheaded solutions that responsible managers regard as too threatening to adopt. (Their general character is discussed below.) Moreover, it is clear that similar problems will arise at other interfaces of the system beta cycle; the third and fourth stages, for example, return us to the points of physical operation and open up the whole field of conflict between those who have to achieve action (stage three), namely, the line management, and those who have to audit or inspect the results of that action (stage four), namely, the staff departments. And the fifth stage of system beta, control, or the confirmation, modification, or rejection of the trial decision that has been taken at the second stage, returns us once more to the higher level of the power structure. At all of these phases in its evolution, the social process of negotiation known as decision-making is likely to be delayed, perverted, or blocked by the communication problems either of authority or of functional differentiation.

Need for Correct Sequencing

It is idle to imagine that a system can be changed, or can develop itself, or, in the language of this book, can learn, if those who are attempting to change it (or to teach it) do not observe the sequence of the system beta cycle. Unless the senior management is willing to accept the full implications of what is assembled in the survey stage, so that any trial decision for action may have its full support, it is a waste of time to attempt the action phase. One cannot permanently change an organization to any marked degree merely by fraternization among those in the lower ranks, although senior management may be less reluctant to take a disagreeable line of action if it is assured that its subordinates are more united in support of it than had been expected. Furthermore, unless the management that makes the trial decision is capable of motivating those who need to act upon it, and is also able to trust those whom it has appointed to inspect or audit the consequences that flow from it, it will be quite unable to judge whether what it is doing is what it set out to do or is of any real value to the organization. The operational paradox may be restated:

System beta demands a cycle of operations that, by its essential nature, tends either to heighten potential communication barriers or to raise fresh ones, between parties essential to operating the cycle. To overcome these communication barriers, all parties, although retaining special interests in particular phases of the cycle, must be brought to a common understanding of the cycle as a whole.

FORMATION OF KEY GROUPS

The visiting fellows, in general, adopted the standard device for resolving this paradox, namely, establishment of one or more groups of persons identified by the fellows as occupying key positions in the different phases of the system beta cycle. These were generally the managers most concerned with the second and third stages of trial decision and action. While there is nothing particularly original in the idea that, faced with the need to change a complex system of which the dynamics and the inertias are imperfectly understood, it is prudent for the manager in charge to consult those involved,[5] it is nevertheless of fresh interest to examine the notion of consultative groups in the light of system beta.

The fellows had begun their diagnoses of the problems offered to them by a program of free interviews, primarily intended to scan the three elements of system alpha (managerial values: "Where is the power in this organization, and for what is it used?"; external system: "What is the environment we are in, and how can it offer scope for what this power wants to achieve?"; and internal system: "What resources does this power command, and how can they be marshaled with best effect?") Such inquiry is the entry to system beta; it develops, still in the first stage, into a more localized analysis as the critical elements in system alpha become more clearly defined. As the survey stage advances, the fellows will be able to tabulate and cross-check their findings; as suggested above, they will be able to verify with considerable effect certain basic strengths and weaknesses, certain agreements and conflicts, certain motivations and resistances. A first organic interpretation of this data, noting the parties who support opposing arguments or even recount contradictory versions of the same supposed facts, will both suggest possible decisions and align the parties in favor of, or in opposition to, these decisions. In what form any particular fellow chooses to present his interpretation, either for his own use or to persuade the management to consider one line of action or another, is not important. Some fellows may use arrays of findings, by persons interviewed and by topics raised; others may keep their notes as in their original time sequence and draw their conclusions impressionistically. But all will begin to see who are the key persons both supporting and acting upon the trial decisions, or opposing or resisting them, and it is these who must be assembled, in the first instance, to discuss specific issues raised by the fellow. Whether they meet as one group or as more than one, with arrangements for keeping effective contact between the different groups, is a matter on which each particular fellow must use his judgment and, should he feel like it, take the advice of parties known to each other to be opposed.

In practice, it is found that, whether or not such groups will come together when invited to do so by some person, such as a visiting fellow, known not to be aligned with any given faction, depends largely upon the support given to the project by the top management. If the president, seconded by the fellow, has succeeded in making it clear for what purpose he is prepared to support the innovative efforts, it is highly likely that all invited will attend, even though it is the intention of some to press for changes that they know will be resisted by others. Indeed, there may even be complaints that not enough persons have been invited, should the word get around that top management means business. Such meetings should de-emphasize the official status of those who attend; all should sit in places allocated at random, and there should be no chairman, only the fellow to introduce what he has to say and to outline the issues on which he wishes to hear the views of others.

His introductory remarks should suggest a meeting of perhaps two hours, divided into his presentation of perhaps fifteen minutes, a perfectly free discussion of perhaps one hour, with the remainder of the time given to the group in answering direct questions put by the fellow. After there is agreement — perhaps not enthusiastically expressed — to some such timetable, the fellow should give a brief presentation of his findings, mentioning how many persons he has seen, what kind of opinions they hold or what facts they contributed; as far as possible, these sources of information should be anonymous and their evidences checked against published policies or statistics. The fellow should then state the problem as he sees it and suggest along what lines he feels the solution of it is to be traced. He should be neither entirely positive nor excessively tentative. Where, in his analysis, he is sure of intelligent unanimity among his listeners, he must emphasize it and then move away from this central rock into the ever deepening waters of uncertainty. He should finish his introductory presentation with a clear statement of what he sees as some ambiguity or uncertainty that all would wish to have resolved or removed. In his opening remarks, he should, as far as possible, avoid all interdepartmental or interlevel divergences; these can be postponed until the group has developed some sense of unity. Nor should the fellow be too diffident. It was a finding of great importance, in the first Inter-University Program, that the managements of the receiving enterprises learned to respect, indeed, in some cases, to envy, the analytical skills exhibited by their visiting fellows who, three months before, knew nothing of the industries in which their hosts were working nor of the strategic problems by which their hosts felt themselves confronted. There seems no reason for an intelligent and experienced visitor to hesitate in outlining his views of the unstructured problems of his host, provided his analysis has been based upon a systematic search of the setting in which the problem is believed to exist. After all, nobody else in the enterprise has had the same opportunities for exploring the managerial maze.

The Agenda for Group Discussion

The members of the group will already be known to the fellow, who will have interviewed them, probably more than once; he may also have met them on committees in the course of their normal business. But it is unlikely that he will have met a majority of them before in face to face groups concerned primarily with his project. There are several reasons why he should now make the most of his chance.

First, if later they are to become involved in taking action together upon strategies largely flowing from his own studies, it is useful for him to do all he can, and as soon as he can, to integrate them into a coherent group, whatever may be the contradictions that are now one reason for him to bring them together. There are many forces that make for group cohesion, but personal knowledge of those with whom one may need to work on shared problems is always one of the more powerful among them. A shrewd observer of the group should thus be able to judge how well integrated its members are already, and therefore to select those tactics most likely to engender the further integration necessary for his project to succeed.

Second, a group meeting gives both the fellow and each individual manager the chance to identify and review any misinterpretations that each may have made of the other's words during their earlier discussions. Those whom the fellow saw at the start of his study may wish to add to what they first said. The group meeting will also offer to the fellow a chance for reassessing what some individuals may have said to him privately. Men with fixed ideas or personal problems may welcome the chance to unload these in front of uncommitted strangers, such as the visiting fellow, but may keep silent about them in front of established colleagues. The group meeting will thus give the fellow some insight into the value of his original observations.

Third, a group meeting called to discuss the meaning of specific evidence will soon give to the fellow some view of the range of motivations, both departmental and personal, among those present. Concrete facts or firmly expressed opinions, brought out before other members of a group involved, or likely to become involved, in practical operations, will soon reveal any divergence of interests within the group. Even more important (certainly from the viewpoint of the fellow hoping to secure, by his experience of a specific project, a wider view of the total system in which the project must be designed and implemented), the meeting of these particular members, wherever they may have been drawn from, may gradually suggest and eventually reveal other and wider conflicts or alliances that are significant in the total setting. A discussion group drawn from different departments but consisting largely of middle managers may not only help to clarify disagreements between, say, sales and production; it may bring out, or throw fresh light upon, conflicts between all middle managers as a class and, say, top management, regional directors, affiliated enterprises, trade unions, and other subsystems of the organism. Without a knowledge of these wider influences, the diagnosis and action proposals of the fellow might be misleadingly inadequate, but, without the help of the group discussion, he might never be able to identify them.

Fourth, members of a group meeting of this kind may discover that they have some room to maneuver (that is, to make minor decisions and to put them into effect) without needing to obtain the authority of their collective superiors. Errors of interpretation of existing procedures or simple blockages of information channels can be discovered and cleared away without the group members' needing to consult other than among themselves. This recognition that they already have some power to help themselves may encourage them to meet again in, say, two months, after bringing before themselves minor issues on their own initiative. Many of the enterprises participating in the Inter-University Program previously had slender means of identifying and solving trivial problems of this kind, and the presence of a visiting fellow, straddling several departments, helped them to cross their traditional frontiers.[6] As one such visitor pointed out: "The organization chart, taken seriously, explains at a glance why and where the blockages exist. In itself, it is the key to understanding why the organization cannot use new ideas. Talk about the Iron Curtain and the Cold War!"

CLIMATES FOR ACTION

Although it has been stressed above that the system beta model must be preserved so that a clear distinction, certainly in logic, is kept between the search for information, on the one hand, and the trial decisions to be made with that information, on the other, the activities of the key discussion group illuminate both stages. Its task is both descriptive and normative; it looks both to what is and to what should be. It helps to clarify the existing facts and to interpret them in the light of possible future decisions. In the same way, while still preserving the logical distinction between the trial decision and the action to be taken upon it (and, once more, because the two stages largely involve different levels of authority), a well-structured key group can do much to prepare the action expected to flow from a trial decision. It was observable that, in the majority of the projects undertaken within the Inter-University Program, a condition critical to success, second in importance only to the support of the top management, was the cooperation, in specific change, of those parts of the organization perhaps not being specifically changed, but nevertheless caught up in the effects of change introduced elsewhere. In other words, searches intended to isolate the seat of trouble, or to circumscribe the springs of innovation, with a program of action directed at these points alone are inevitably condemned to fail. Action by any one person at any one time may well be specific to that person at that time, but its success for the organization as a whole depends upon the cooperation of others. Since these others may well be inconvenienced by the effects of remote events, particularly if they also are competitors for resources implicitly within the same budget, these problems of cooperation in action are far from easy. Internecine war is the most destructive war of all, and it is immature to believe that it can be avoided by general appeals for loyalty to the organization as a whole. The same key group, whose members have already learned to discuss and interpret the findings of a visiting fellow in terms of possible trial decisions, is a helpful managerial instrument for reconciling specific local action with general organic support. It is a question of trade: What bargains can be struck? The fellow, with his external vision, may be able to suggest some negotiable deals.

Overtures to Action

Every effort to resolve this innovation paradox must be almost entirely situational. Who is the prime mover, or client, who are his likely allies, who are the neutrals, and who are the opponents? The list will vary with each case and can be determined only in the here and now of operational reality. But our experience in the score of projects that, in the Inter-University Program, were levered toward effective action, suggests that certain behavioral questions should be posed at the action stage of any project intended to change an existing state of affairs. The visiting fellow has an advantage in posing them, because he is not seen as competing for permanent power or status within the new situation that he is helping his client to bring about. Whether the questions are put to the key groups as they were originally set up to clarify the processes of search, whether the groups are now to be reinforced by representatives

of specifically action-oriented interests such as production supervisors, or whether these questions are posed during the original
search and interpretation sessions are alike matters on which
the visiting fellow needs to exercise his judgment and his past
experience. Our present task is to identify those questions that
seemed most effective in bringing out and resolving the inhibi-
tions against action.

The fellow must make known, in due course, when he is
encouraging the group to search for solutions together; he will
need to say this openly if he has previously called the group
together merely to interpret his interviews with them, a purpose
seen as less threatening than to take responsibility, however
limited, for the design and implementation of programs of
effective action. As soon as he is sure that his new direction has
been appreciated, he can begin to explore the attitudes of those
present toward operational change. The following questions
may suggest some of the fears and doubts most often uncovered
during the first Inter-University Program.

- What demands already made on people in the key group
  are felt to be unreasonable or conflicting?
- What present services, including information about objectives, results, and resources, are felt to be inadequate or
  inappropriate for handling these demands?
- What standards of achievement (if these are known) do
  the group members' superiors expect of them?
- How do they evaluate their own abilities and powers to meet
  these standards?
- To what extent do they feel that their present problems are
  known to, or are of concern to, their superiors?
- If they feel that, on such questions as those above, they are
  not in effective touch with their superiors, to what extent
  do they see themselves as responsible for the gap?
- What preparatory action do they consider necessary before
  any new policies are introduced? What, if any, present
  activities could be dispensed with?

Questions such as these may exist in their own right; they need not be specifically concerned with particular future operations. Nevertheless, to pose them may be cardinal to introducing any change, by bringing out possible sources of resistance to any fresh proposals. It was discovered that, in about half the cases, the mere raising of these questions was enough to answer them from within the resources of the groups themselves; in the other cases, the fellows were generally able to convince the senior managers for whom they worked (the clients) that some attention should be paid to what the key groups already had to say before much could be done to advance fresh plans for action.

Problems of Inspection and Control

The fourth and fifth stages of system beta are, to a large extent, special cases of the first and second. In the fourth stage, of inspecting or auditing the outcome of a given action, the search process is no longer general; it is aimed at measuring specific anticipated parameters and, what is even more precise, at measuring them against standards already laid down. If the results actually achieved differ significantly from those expected, it may be possible for particular individuals to trace both the causes of divergence and the corrective action to take to deal with them. But in general there is no one-dimensional source of deviation, and the key group may prove again to be an instrument for wider understanding. In the fifth stage, the responsible decision-makers are faced with the task of confirming, amending, or rejecting their previous trial decisions, so that the involvement of the key group can again provide useful support. Many of the problems of authority and communication noted in the discussion of the second stage of trial decision will recur at the final stage of control, except that, should the deviations from what was expected be both significant and negative, the key group may need to withstand severe tensions. Yet it is exactly in these conditions, making for stress, that the need for the key group is greatest; it is also in these conditions that the organization is best able to learn. Indeed, the quality of a successful leader is most readily expressed in any review of progress that he carries through with his colleagues. If it is a review to which all contribute and from which he himself may be seen to learn, he need have no fear about the development of his enterprise as a whole.

Generality of Key Groups

Practically every fellow found the key group to be an effective instrument both for helping to interpret their own first impressions drawn from individual interviews and for setting up a variety of action groups at the later operational stages; some fellows found useful a hierarchy of key groups, at the level of the board and its officers, on the one hand, and among the middle managers, on the other. Some groups were interdepartmental and very general, for instance, to trace how, in the past, ideas had passed among sales, research, and production and how, in the future, they could so pass more effectively. Other groups were highly specialized, to discuss the circulation of information among departments, or even to compare departments according to the cultural differences among their decision criteria.

In the course of this activity, it became clear that here was an essential instrument of organizational learning, a group of persons not normally forming a mutually responsible operational team, able to accept as items for discussion a series of points raised by an observer neutral in his first approach and striving, within his personal loyalty to his client, to remain objective in his continued engagement. A well-chosen group, serviced by a visiting fellow, performs three functions: It supplies facts and opinions that many of its members are normally too busy to procure on their own; it opens communications that may normally be tightly blocked; and it provides opportunities for constructive discussion that are rarely offered with any other method. These may be obvious truths, but for that very reason they are readily forgotten. In our preoccupation with the vast problems of a restless and unaccommodating age, we forget the basic questions, such as: How does a man use his known abilities? How may he enhance, by creativity, the talents that are still latent within him? How does a traditional management replace the fading power of authoritarian coercion with the growing power of the multidisciplinary team? It is to such questions that, inside the framework of system beta, we seek to address ourselves. But it was during the interplay of personal hopes and fears, on the one hand, with organizational strength and weakness, on the other, that both the men themselves and their mutual relations were changed, and, it is to be supposed, changed for the better, because the dynamics of such change were the subject of review. From our studies of this interplay were developed the concepts of system gamma, notions of managerial symbiosis developed elsewhere in this book.

REVIEW OF ROLE OF VISITING FELLOWS

It need not now be emphasized that the role of the visiting fellow is both singular and ambiguous. But, if a condition helpful to institutional learning is the advice of an observer but marginally implicated in the power struggles of the enterprise, we are justified in asking where the candidates for this role are to be found and trained on any significant scale. It should be by now reasonably clear why relative independence is essential, but, in view of the issues that any discussion of it immediately raises, it may be well to list some of the reasons.

· An independent observer, despite his formal commitment to his client, is seen neither as competing for career advantage or benefit with any particular person inside the receiving enterprise nor as a confident expert ready at all times with advice on which his listeners are expected to act; this ensures a high level of objectivity in search and interpretation.

· Such relative independence also grants a moral stature; even though this must be used with discretion, a mature and intelligent fellow can, in his own way, interpret, for single individuals, for a key group, for his own client, or even for the top management of an enterprise the course of their behavior; he can suggest, for example, that they are, knowingly or not, either deceiving themselves or exploiting vital issues for purely personal reasons or have embarked upon courses of action of questionable social outcome; in so expressing himself he may risk conflict, but he increases the independence of his role.

·By remembering this primary role as a student of management problems rather than by emphasizing the strength drawn from his privileged position, the visiting fellow will help to engender within the staff of his receiving enterprise a like interest in its own learning processes.

· The visiting fellow remains at all times in close contact, both through his own university group of three or four other fellows and through all the fellows in the program, with a score of similar projects developing elsewhere; in this way he provides not only himself but also his receiving enterprise with a multiple stream of new ideas about its members and their tasks.

These reasons, among others, may well explain the need to have on hand, both for industry and for public administration, a fund of independent agents, whether as fellows produced in the Inter-University Program or provided in other ways. It is essential to return to the question: Where are they to be found and trained? The question leads to another: What are the developmental processes of any particular institution? And this question, in turn, raises a further one: If the developmental processes of a particular institution are only one aspect of the wider processes of social development and cultural growth, what is the interest of the establishments of learning, notably, the universities, in these wider processes and in their specific applications to particular industrial or social systems?

We cannot enter into this interesting question here, but, in the view of the majority of fellows, the Inter-University Program has raised the following propositions in higher education; it will apparently require new forms of universities for these propositions to be worked out, and this working out will itself provide the kinds of help that, in the Inter-University Program, were supplied largely by the visiting fellows.

Propositions in Higher Education

·The universities, through the next decade, should give sustained critical attention to the nature of their social role. They should review their involvement in social growth,

8

particularly to anticipate, to study, and to influence the effects of social change under the impact of an accelerating technology. They should ask if their (descriptive) tradition as seekers after, and purveyors of, knowledge should not be extended to encourage the (normative) use of that knowledge not only by individuals but also by organizations and institutions as such. They should, for example, not only help to prepare the individual doctor for his career; they should also help the health services in which he is to work to prepare for and to meet their own future needs in relation to society as a whole.

· Given the rate at which teachable knowledge is growing and the rate at which social institutions of all kinds are changing, the university should see its primary role not as providing instruction to immature adolescents but as providing persons at all stages of their lives both with the opportunities to learn and with knowledge of how to employ those opportunities to develop their learning abilities still further. The present system of entry at, or around, the age of eighteen years, for the vast majority, must be amended to offer to mature persons courses, such as the Inter-University Program, of substantial length, in order that they may reorganize their perceptions of past experiences and thereby contribute to the development of the university itself. In the design and conduct of these courses, the normal distinctions between staff and students should be fundamentally reconsidered.

· Such opportunities are conveniently offered through the performance of useful project work, whether in industry, commerce, government, social institutions, or elsewhere, including the running of the university itself. Such projects should be concerned with defining the objectives of social or industrial institutions and with designing real systems for achieving these objectives in responsible cooperation with the people in charge of the institutions.

· At every stage of their life within the university community, all its members should be encouraged to evaluate what they may be doing by what they themselves judge to be its outcome. No activity, particularly in science or technology, should be judged except in relation to its perceived social need and social purpose sought in open debate. All academic disciplines should be encouraged to seek integration with the life sciences and with the social sciences, so that the university, within the limits of its vision, may be able organically to understand, and responsibly to advise upon, the long-term social effects that may flow from developing these disciplines.

· The relation of the university to government should be reviewed. If the university is to take a responsible share in the design of public services, it must be in contractual relationship with government. It must also retain some independence of government in case its analysis of a social issue — for example, the growth of urban crime — might suggest that government policy is seriously inadequate or even misconceived. Such seeming contradictions demand that, in some countries, the present basis of university administration may need revision.

It is for those at present in charge of the universities to debate these and similar propositions. Knowledge has become both a drug and a high explosive, and the time has come to examine the social role of the industry that deals in it.

OBSERVATIONS ON INDUSTRIAL DEMOCRACY

These observations on the processes of social negotiation here reflected in what has been called system beta may seem, to the student of industrial politics, thin stuff. In this democratic age, it may be argued, there are, or should be, less circuitous methods of harnessing the energies of man. Industrial democracy has a long history and takes many forms; my experience of it extends from trying to set up the consultative committees of the British coal industry, both before and after nationalization, to analyzing problems of motivation and productivity in countries behind the iron curtain. In all of these instances — whether we are concerned with democratization of ownership, as in Poland or Rumania, in a nationalized industry in Britain, or even in a scheme of business copartnership; with democratization of administration, as with doctors serving on hospital management committees or with German trade-unionists on organs of

Mitbestimmung; or with democratization of contract, as with workers' representatives serving on statutory wages councils, including teachers on the Burnham Committee—the necessity remains for cooperation among those responsible for getting things done. It is immensely important to recognize that neither democratization of ownership nor of administration nor of contract, alone or together, is adequate to secure this essential involvement in the management process. This involvement is a situational input and must be specifically treated as such. Action cannot be taken in general terms; it always was, is, and always will be dependent on its conditions and on those who take it. We need to know more than we do about its nature.

Perhaps the Inter-University Program has made, in its own way, three modest contributions to this knowledge: It has provided an institutional mechanism, in the exchange of senior managers, for examining the wider context of the need for, and implications of, organizational change; it has suggested, in system beta and the key group, a formula for introducing such change; and it has identified the need for bringing an analysis of the general change process, together with the training of people to catalyze it, into the normal course of university studies and research. It is intended specifically to emphasize these three points in the future development of the program, both in Belgium and elsewhere.

NOTES

1. See Figure 2.
2. See p. 135 for a reference to learning and management by analogy.
3. This opinion is based upon some unpublished researches conducted at the University of Manchester; the basic need, for innovation to succeed, seems to be that at least one member of the most powerful coalition within the enterprise so strongly believes in the new idea that his colleagues are convinced by his sincerity, and are also sure that he can carry responsibility for dealing with the disturbances that its introduction will create. Generally the paradox is not properly resolved because powerful members of the leading coalition do not see it as their task to effect coordination at the departmental level. But given a top manager seized of the integrating problems and also committed to the principle behind the new project, the paradox may prove relatively insubstantial.
4. In a further development of the educational principle of exchanging senior managers in order to analyze more realistically the basic problems of an

enterprise, a consortium of presidents of Egyptian enterprises was brought to recognize its key role in these affairs. The presidents agreed that, from the very start of the exchange program, each would act as chairman of the *structure d'acceuil* in his own enterprise, giving one half-day every two weeks to helping his visiting fellow collect, interpret, and apply the evidence on which his project was founded. No less intelligently, they also agreed to a regular program of conferences among, and supportive of, themselves, for each to face more confidently the stresses inherent in learning from an independent observer what may actually be going on within his dominions.

5. Justinian (ca. 550) left us a famous maxim: "Matters that concern all should be agreed by all"; that he himself rarely observed it is neither here nor there for our present argument.

6. During the occupation of the administrative block by students at the University of Manchester, England, early in 1970, it was discovered that there was no way for staff and students to negotiate with each other except through the courts of law. A local priest, in a letter published by *The Guardian,* offered his mediatory services to both parties, thus reviving the appropriately medieval notion of sanctuary. A few months later, similar offers were made by local clergy, during the seven-week-long dispute at Pilkingtons, the leading British glass manufacturers. This was a three-cornered affair, involving management, workers, and trade union, all of whom were shown to have no rational means of negotiating with the others until incalculable harm had been done. The final mediator, like Theodore Roosevelt intervening in the Russo-Japanese War, was the "Emperor of All the Unions," Victor Feather, speaking from his palace in London, nearly two hundred miles away.

4

Adaptation and Learning

An individual may be said to have learned when his behavior after the learning occasion remains significantly different from his behavior before. Since a central theme of this book is education, it is desirable to make explicit the theory of learning—such as it may be—on which the Inter-University Program is based. Since, moreover, it is about the education of managers, the theory of learning must be relevant to the tasks of managers. System gamma has been devised to establish this relevance.

This chapter discusses the structure of adaptation and tries to relate it to such characteristic activities of the manager as decision-making and action, both routine and creative; communication with others; self-awareness and awareness of others; and, very sketchily, relates the model employed, system gamma, to other theories of learning. It suggests that there are probably four kinds of action or creativity—under magic, imagination, empiricism, and design—and that these form a sequence of maturing sophistication: magic characterizing childhood, imagination characterizing adolescence, empiricism characterizing practical maturity, and design, the depersonalized objectivity of abstract truth.

100

It is suggested that managers are principally concerned with establishing what they should do (design, system alpha), with working out the sequence of how they should do it (negotiation, system beta), and with adapting themselves to the new situations so brought about (learning, system gamma). Management is an action-oriented trade, and learning among managers aims, it may be supposed, to develop the capacity to act more effectively as the result of experience.

In the hierarchy of different kinds of learning described by Gagne,[1] policy formation would evidently take the highest rank, for it is even more complex than problem solving; the strategist has first to define his problems before trying to solve them. There is, moreover, no set of canonical solutions to a policy problem; the acceptability of different solutions depends upon the value systems of those called upon to approve these solutions. But if, in this sense, the definition of the objective— to learn how to be systemic in policy formation—is elusive and vague, it can be made more precise by declaring the nature of the particular system and subsystems around which the policy forming process is to be built.

Nevertheless, to appear to clarify the objectives by stating them in terms of systems alpha and beta as aids to management behavior must not be allowed to deceive even the most enthusiastic supporters. The task is very complex, and it is doubtful whether this (or any other) so-called theory of learning can be more than a structure convenient for classifying the large number of general ideas on which the program has drawn.

Nothing more is claimed for this theory than its use as a frame of reference. In particular, the theory, such as it may be, although making the definition of the managers' value system the first point in its catalogue of components, has nothing directly to say on the merits of particular value systems. It is, to that extent, as amoral as are the scientific ideas on which it purports to draw; although it pretends to examine the development of human beings, it presents no handholds for moral philosophers, although it makes considerable reference to the need for managers to listen to what other persons are trying to say to them.

System gamma, however, tries to avoid simple eclecticism; it is not an impulse choice like that of the housewife in the supermarket, picking from the shelf whatever, on the instant, she feels would be good to take home. It is an attempt to build a consistent and unambiguous set of relationships, both necessary and sufficient, to explain what it is that a manager is doing — and what is being done to the manager — whenever he sets out to influence the course of events that pass to some extent under his influence. It is only out of concern for the visible consequence of what the manager does and of how he is influenced, both in very practical terms, that we are rash enough to seek an appropriate systemic model in the first place, and immodest enough to declare that in system gamma we may have produced one.

There is no attempt here, for example, to identify the philosophical nature of "the course of events that pass to some extent under his (the manager's) influence." Nor is there theorization about the nature of recognition or perception; there is nothing here about the neural circuits that enable ideas to be associated, nor about the programs of search and compilation appropriate for drawing and holding ideas in the forefront of the consciousness. If there were a demand for a complete theory of managerial learning, it would need to take a stand upon these vital questions. However, system gamma is not intended to be an exhaustive treatise on the behavior of men trying to make the best job they can of guiding an incompletely understood present into an even less completely predictable future. It is a set of ideas that has grown out of the struggles of a score of action-oriented managers with a score of open-ended questions. If it is to be judged at all it should be by its appropriateness to our first need: How should managers be encouraged to learn from what they do?

On this account, although system gamma calls for a wide variety of components, and although it touches upon such general questions as the verbal nature of a rational decision, its presentation here is hardly intended to be part of a complete theory of human action. For the present, it is quite sufficient if, by using system gamma, in their discussions among themselves no less than in planning their work within their projects, the fellows get on better than they would have without it. Suffice it to say that system gamma, however complex in itself, is a convenient framework for one very specific task analysis, namely, the project as a medium for taking exercise in the processes of policy formation.

THE IMPACT OF EVENTS

A manager lives under the constant assault of events; some of these may have no observable effect upon him, some a temporary effect, some an effect that is permanent, or even regenerative. A regenerative effect may be defined as so concentrating the attention that the manager seeks to identify its cause, and thereby to make more use of it.[2] Thus an event, defined very broadly as an opinion or fact expressed in conversation, a happening in the factory, an altercation in the board room, the logic of a financial report or even as an arbitrary inspiration within the manager's own mind, is postulated as making some observable impact either upon what the manager already knows, upon who the manager already is, or upon how the manager already acts. For the present, it is enough to consider the impact of the event upon the manager's current activity; this is probably to find some satisfactory course of action to relieve the pressure of his current problems, a course of partial escape that some optimists call problem solving. However this may be, the search for such relief demands that the manager has some grasp of system alpha (p. 33). Even if they are not held in the forefront of his consciousness, the manager seeking either to escape from his troubles or to seize upon his opportunities must be clear about the three elements of the system alpha paradigm, namely,

> "By what set of values am I guided?
> What is blocking their fulfillment?
> What can I do against the blockage?"

or   "By what set of values am I guided?
                  What is this chance to fulfill them?
                  What can I do to seize the chance?"

The system alpha paradigm demands that the manager understand his motivation, his problem, and his tools. Thus, his motivation to act is the system alpha value element that gives meaning to his task, and he must know what this is. In operational terms, he must be able to explain to those around him what he is trying to achieve as a manager. Figure 1 suggests, for a number of typical situations of achievement, the appropriate sets of three elements. It is clear that Figure 1 is grossly oversimplified, and that, even in the starkest illustrations, the decision values are not one alone, but a complex hierarchy.

The impact of the event that induces learning may be of any order of magnitude. If it is sufficiently striking (as must have been the first discovery of gunpowder) the manager may pause in what he is doing to note what he finds of interest; he may even set out to act upon it at the very moment. It is shown later that managers differ widely in their predisposing states of mind toward new experiences of this kind; the power of creativity or of inventiveness seems to be born of the capacity to notice, and of the curiosity to enlist, unusual events occurring in one's real world. However, it may be supposed that the impact of the event upon the previous condition of the manager has momentarily produced within him a new condition, questioning an old belief, raising a fresh hope, exploring a new opportunity, assessing a new resource. This new condition will, to the action-oriented man, suggest some new practice, some fresh line of attack on a problem, a change of strategy or of tactics; it may suggest a new relation between things that he had never previously seen as connected, or that he had always believed to be related in some other way. Stated simply, the manager has a new idea.

Possibilities of Response

One as cautious as the average manager will not normally

stake his reputation nor his security upon an idea alone. He will
want to assure himself that the idea is likely to work, particularly
before proposing it to his superior, should their relations be
at all uncertain. It is not unknown for men with new ideas to
give up their jobs in order to be free to develop their inspiration
elsewhere. In general, as the difficulty of engendering change
in European industry proclaims, many new ideas must be condemned without any form of trial. Several fellows were struck
by the arrangements made by American enterprises to seek out
new ideas from within themselves, such as brainstorming
lunches for branch or factory managers, trouble-shooting com-
missions composed largely of recent graduates and frequent
staff rotations inspired by the hope of cross-fertility. In Europe,
on the other hand, the widespread lack of long-range plans
and of corporate strategies, so far from stimulating new ideas
at the lower managerial levels, give some fellows the impression
of actually inhibiting them. But should an idea really impress
him, the prudent manager, with the professional qualifications
linked to higher education common in Western Europe, will
seek and eventually find a convenient opportunity for testing
it. He will pay attention to the outcome of this test, and he will
try to evaluate within this outcome any effects that might have
been caused by other influences.

If, for example, a new step in some manufacturing process
promises to reduce factory costs, the insightful manager will
wish to satisfy himself that any reduction achieved cannot in
fact be attributed to any other variable such as changes of, say,
raw materials, of the quality of supervision, of the volume
produced, or to any other adventitious reason. He will, in other
words, inspect or audit the outcome (such as by variance analysis
inside a standard costing system) of trying his new idea out in
practice before finally adopting it, before modifying it by
further trials, or before rejecting it altogether.

This total process may be illustrated as a cycle of

1. An attention-fixing event occurring within a framework of
   experience

2. A new constructive relationship perceived in or around this event
3. An attempt to exploit this relationship for some desired purpose
4. An audit or inspection of the results of this exploitation
5. The incorporation (or not) of the relationship into the experience of the manager, namely, a process of learning

This is system beta; it has already been shown as the lowest row in Figure 5 (p. 50), and we take this visual reference to the flow process as an opportunity for emphasizing the inner structure of our argument.

Learning is not an acquisition of the new knowledge so much as a rearrangement of the old. We try, by taking repeated action, to build, out of what we already know, those successive programs of behavior that enable us, with increasing accuracy, to predict their outcomes.

The system beta paradigm, as applied to the response of a manager, may be that anticipated from a prudent man anxious to know whether, in practice, his actions, based upon his beliefs, contribute to the solution of his system alpha problems. But a very large number of persons act without going through all the steps of the system beta cycle.[3] Not even all professional managers are as rational, (as concerned with verifying that outcome matches anticipation) as is suggested by this cycle. Further on is a description of several other types of behavior among action takers, and these types fall short, in identifiable degrees, of that set forth in the complete five-stage cycle suggested previously.

Applying System Beta to Practice

As has been emphasized, the manager's world is one of action. Some outcome observable by others must follow each test of his new knowledge. This outcome he could announce in advance; he could explain to others his forecasts in terms of system alpha. But such terms would be personal to himself: the values important to *him, his* perception of the problem and *his* estimate of the resources available to treat it. Other expert observers might make different judgments on any of these elements, but all with courage enough could be invited to state their individual predictions accordingly, namely, to build their own system-beta cycles. Their forecasts could then be compared with the observable outcomes. The test of such different prognostications is an everyday occurrence at the racetrack, where the difference of view among the forecasters is settled by the order in which the horses are, by independent judges, observed to finish. However, in management one cannot afford every time to await the outcome of one's native and untutored intuition; one must recognize in advance and correct for at the times the natural biases likely to be carried into each forecasting situation.

This molding of the managerial consciousness is provided by a continuous interaction with other managers, as suggested in Figures 4, 6, and 7; it is symbiotic. If A discusses his perception of X with B, it is inescapable that B offers his perception of X to A. The discussion may then modify the views of both A and B, although not necessarily to improve their correspondence with reality. The chance of actual improvement further and inescapably demands both action and audit, and the success of any system-beta cycle, intended to mold the managers's world in terms of his chosen system alpha, must itself depend upon the manager's personal success in clarifying his own vision of the world, which system alpha might reform. Thus every manager out to improve his abilities needs feedback, not against objective reality alone, *but also against the interpretation by others of his own behavior.* Such mutual lessons in self-awareness provide the essence of system gamma.

In this systemic representation of the manager's experience, the concept of feedback, of comparing results with expectation, of evaluating the impact of his action upon the reality situation, is of crucial importance. Without knowledge of results there can be no *internally directed* change of behavior, and, for the effective development of managers, learning must be considered as internally directed, even if the motivating idea is not internally generated, but is adventitious or even copied from or dictated by another person. Behavior temporarily changed under duress,

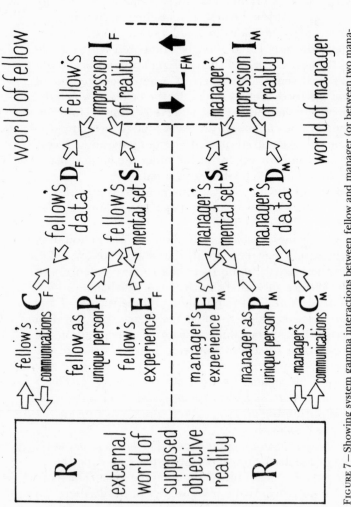

FIGURE 7 – Showing system gamma interactions between fellow and manager (or between two managers) during identification of field problem.

This is an extension of what is shown as the sub-system beta interaction of Figure 6, which in turn reflects the structure of Figure 4. But Figure 6 does not show that the "managerial reporting channels" are merely a collection of human beings having the same basic structures of personality and ... as the fellow. Each of these human beings (managers) brings into his discussions with the ...

such as political conformity exacted by machine guns, is not internally directed. The occasions of the machine guns may be remembered, but the responses displayed during them are not permanently assimilated.

To admit the need for men to pause from time to time as they press forward, in order to check what they are doing, to secure some knowledge of their results, to seek feedback in accordance with the latest doctrines of cybernetics, seems often to be thought of as one more defeatist modernism, or as a sign that the generation has lost confidence in itself, or as one more delaying tactic, yet another restrictive practice. They may ask, "Do we no longer have minds of our own?" In some senses it is certainly new, particularly in those forms of group psychodynamics deliberately created for friends to tell each other how unpleasant they can be when they set their minds to it. The goal-seeking devices within automatic pilots and other servomechanisms, are also relatively modern, having their origin in Watts' centrifugal governor. But the notion that the human being owes his development to an awareness of his own behavior is of great antiquity indeed, as may be read in the following from The Book of Proverbs:

Reprove not a scorner lest he hate thee: rebuke a wise man and he will love thee. Give instruction to a wise man and he will be wiser: teach a just man and he will increase in learning.[4]

The wisdom of the prudent is to understand his way: but the folly of fools is deceit. The simple believeth every word: but the prudent man looketh well to his going. The simple inherit folly: but the prudent are crowned with knowledge.[5]

The author of these lines had little to learn from system beta or from the teachings of modern psychology.

It is not difficult to suggest physical mechanisms that at one level or another simulate the consolidating effects of self-knowledge, of seeing more objectively the results of one's actual behavior contrasted with one's anticipated behavior, of recognizing that one's image seen by others may differ from the image held of the self. The theory of alternating current, for example, is rich in propositions about resonance, and the wave theory of light explains anomalous dispersion, a resonance effect, in terms of the same second-order differential equations. It is now known that the brain is a source of electrical rhythms, so it would not be surprising if the phenomena of resonance turned out to be critical in learning. If the frequency patterns of anticipation (stage two fed forward) are very similar to those of observed response (stage four fed back) there may be reinforcement by resonance within the memory circuits; if there are significant differences between the frequency patterns of anticipation and effect there is no resonance and no memory. But we do not undertake to offer proposals to neurologists. Nor do we forget that consciousness and differential equations are not exactly interchangeable aspects of some common experience.

Relations to Other Theories of Learning

The system model of Figure 5 could hardly be simpler; moreover, Figure 2 shows that it follows from the nature of system alpha, and even system alpha can be further simplified into the most basic system of all, namely the relation of one entity to another. If the internal resources represent the first entity and the external opportunities represent the second, and the value system contained within the internal resources represents the stored experience of the interaction between them, then system alpha is merely a statement that an organism and its environment interact. The learning model is thus growing very metaphysical, almost a specimen of the self-evident propositions inherited from the eighteenth century. It becomes, therefore, desirable to relate it to other theories of learning found in the psychological literature.

Any such review should start with the work of Thorndike,[6] and although he says little about system alpha or about symbiosis, it is evident that system beta is not much more than his early laws of readiness, exercise, and response, here integrated and extended into a universal paradigm. Even when he has changed these laws into action tendencies (the event urging the manager to do something), into the laws of use and of disuse (repeated practice making the manager more able to take the action), and into the law of effect (success strengthening and failure weakening the manager's inclination and skill to take the action), the similarity persists. Also, because system gamma, of which system beta is only a part, might claim, with further development, to suggest a global theory of human action, it should submit itself to the general questions to be leveled at all learning theories. These include the following.

1. *Does Learning Occur by Reinforcement or by Association?*

The answer is plain. The subject must see the effect of his behavior by comparing outcome with expectation. Mere association by argument, analogy, or Cartesian logic[7] is inadequate for system gamma. Thus it is that the presidents and other senior managers of the enterprises in the Inter-University Program are unanimous in their emphasis upon its superiority over the traditional seminars that they have been loyally supporting for more than a decade; and thus it is that the university management centers of Belgium are, as a result of their experience in this program, reconsidering their traditional methods of teaching. Association may be given a veneer of reinforcement by discussion and some learning may result, but it is not what is taught by the emotional annealing of responsible action leading to imperative and observable consequences.

2. *Does Learning Occur Suddenly or in Small Increments?*

The meaning of the words "learning" and "increments" must be examined to interpret the question. The design of the program in its time-sequence was, in a sense, a reflection of system beta; the learning process displays the same temporal order. The introductory courses (of reading and advice, of skills in interviewing, systems analysis, model building, and so forth) were seen solely as orientation toward the main item, namely, the project itself. The eight months (or longer) to be spent full time on this was divided, by the visit to America, into a diagnostic phase of four months and an action phase of the

9

same length. The diagnostic phase, in principle, embraced not only the necessary surveys (stage one of system beta) but also the formulation of the trial strategies (stage two) that were presented for criticism to the American experts. These proposals, in turn, anticipated the actions to be started by the fellows in their host enterprises after their return to Europe (stage three), as well as the setting up of the necessary audit services to judge whether or not the proposals were likely to be effective (stage four). Thus the action phase continued the cycle with stages three and four of system beta. Stage five was mainly embodied in the learning processes of the fellows, with the agreement of their presidents, through the consolidation of their experience by part-time return visits, after the fellows had returned to their own enterprises. Indeed, in some cases, it was upon the active insistence of the presidents that their own fellow, having already gained so much from the first four stages, should now see how far his host enterprise was able to generalize from its project experience.

It should thus have been possible throughout the eight months to record the progress of the fellows and to have estimated from these records the depth of their learning at various critical points. However artificial the analogy between the system beta of Figure 5 and the four stages within the eight months spent on the project, there is no doubt that the morale of the group on average, was highest at the end of the two months following their return from America, that is, at the peak of what on paper was supposed to be the main action phase. The discoveries by the fellows that, armed with a set of plans based not only on traditional indices but also on a rational analysis of the subjective opinions (value systems) of their host managements, they were actually able to secure high-level support for action, and also that, in the majority of cases, more was being expected by their hosts from their interventions than the fellows had ever thought possible, raised their spirits to the highest level.

Even the three or four fellows who found themselves up against resistances to their suggestions from the top managements of their host enterprises were less disheartened than they

imagined they would have been. They at least had the satisfaction of knowing that, although their hosts would not follow
their action proposals directly, the principles upon which those
proposals were framed had in all cases been taken over by the
top management to be worked into alternative strategies of
their own. Indeed, to accept with good grace such a transformation of one's efforts might even, in accordance with the latest
ideas of the virtues of cognitive dissonance, have been a blessing
in disguise. Too easy a victory may not much instruct the victor,
and empires established on a single battle rarely endure.

Thus, it can be concluded that, taken in the round, the learning of the fellows, at least in their conviction that they had put
themselves in command of an effective approach to unstructured problems, came relatively suddenly. The encouragement
they received from the American experts certainly brought them
back to Europe filled with confidence; in a real sense, their dress
rehearsals, those presentations before the faculty at M.I.T. and
Harvard, as well as before the experts of the big companies,
were an ordeal by dialectical feedback in itself, a tempering in
the flames of a priori criticism, a preparation for stages three
and four of system beta, sufficient to discover any verbal or
other logical weakness predisposingly fatal to later action. But
it was not until they had tried out in the field their own proposals, and had suddenly discovered, by *operational* feedback their
relevance both to action itself and to the wishes of their hosts,
that the majority were convinced that they now commanded an
integrated system through which to envision and apply their
experience and their skills. To this extent, therefore, the final
act of enlightenment was instantaneous.

In further support of the argument, there is no doubt that
during the first weeks of the diagnostic stage the morale of the
fellows was correspondingly low; they could not believe that the
methods of systems analysis to which they had been introduced
had much relevance to the practical problems in their new industrial environments. As they began to perceive that their novel
methods of survey and structure enabled them, however, actually to take the lead in discussions with their host managers,
their morale rose; at least they could see that they had learned

something about collecting and assembling data that gave them a local advantage—even on questions of fact—over those who should themselves have been the experts as measured by their experience, their involvement, and their responsibility. Thus there was an increment of learning in advance of the enlightenment that followed their first major attempts at action.

Quite evidently, much deeper research is needed; subjectively, at least, it seems as if insight is an instantaneous phenomenon, but since what needs to be learned is in itself almost infinitely granulated in structure (for each stage of any system beta must be treated by the system beta paradigm itself, ad infinitum) the question as to whether total learning, as the sum of many smaller insights, is sudden or continuous turns out to be more than a little ambiguous. To ask by what steps any student managers are to learn remains, nevertheless, a useful question to put to all program designers and to their teachers.

3. Is Learning a Single Factor or a Multifactor Process?

How many different kinds of learning are there? Is association learning, as in case-study arguments, different from reinforcement learning? This question is discussed further on page 134; the answer given by the proposed theory seems to depend upon how many stages of the system beta cycle are completed in the learning process. There are four corresponding *levels* of learning and these may be related to individual development and to the prevailing culture.

4. On What Kind of Intervening Variables Does the Learning Theory Depend?

It is evident, from an inspection of Figure 6, that system gamma depends on a substantial arsenal of intervening concepts. Some of these can, at one level, be explicitly set forth, such as system alpha, the design of a strategy helpful in increasing some objective function, or other aspects of the managerial value system. But within these rather Pythagorean paradigms themselves there are invoked some difficult concepts. What is a value system? Is there such a thing?[8] What is it that, in forming system beta, the manager projects forward as a trial decision from stage two through the simulated action at stage three to be assessed by a simulated audit at stage four, and thereafter compared with itself back at stage two? None can tell; our own consciousness is too elusive for description and the consciousness of others must escape us absolutely. All one is aware of is that certain present conversations with other people have future outcomes which, in one's experience, bear a relation to the reality that they foresee.

Likewise with system gamma as a model for describing our mental imagery, and for comparing one's impressions with those of others. It is hardly important to prove whether the intervening variables of, say, tentative plan, simulated action, subjective evaluation, conjectural creativity, feedforward and feedback, and, indeed, cognitive patterns in general, have any meaning or not, because meaning itself need not be defined. The question is not of meaning, but of utility. Are the concept of system gamma, and the subtle subconcepts it both demands and multiplies, *useful* in developing managers? Beyond this it is not necessary to go, and, what is more, if one did it would only be to find oneself laboring among the problems, alike inexplicable and insoluble, of pattern recognition, cerebral storage circuity, mechanisms for memory search, and, eventually, of the structure of matter and of the nature of space and time. For the present, it is enough to concentrate on improving system gamma as a guide to practical action.

It can be asked how far system beta is related, not to concepts used in general learning theory, but to specific theories of learning. These appear to fall into four classes:

1. Mimesis, or imitation, as the kitten learns by copying the actions of its mother in chasing mice
2. Insight, or simulation, wherein the learner makes an intellectual model of the reality situation and traces a valid result by rational argument, even though this may be below the level of consciousness, doing so, moreover, without suggestion or help from others (a valid result is one that

preserves throughout a one-to-one correspondence to reality)
3. Trial and error, or watching what occurs in practice, either to an action suggestion about or to a random attack upon some undesirable situation
4. Instruction, or following up intelligible clues or questions posed by others already conscious of the final outcome, or to whom the field of learning is already well structured

It is seen that the four classes of learning theory are variations of the system beta cycle shown in Figure 5. In mimesis the new idea suggesting the try-out in practice is not generated by the learner but copied from some trusted example; that is, the pattern of response is not internally designed but ritualistically followed. An act of recognition is, of course, presupposed: by copying its mother, the kitten learns to chase mice and to run away from dogs; the student of economics learns that sometimes he must give different answers to the same question, according to the professor who poses it. The total situation, of question and questioner together, must be recognized before the selected response is made. Nevertheless, the concept of mimesis is quite intelligible in terms of Figure 5; instead of evolving at the second stage of system beta one's own draft action plan for try-out at the third, some established ritual is copied from another person with whom intimate identification exists.

Second, insight is the use of the total model of Figure 5 in an imaginative act of simulation, or of symbolic or verbal representation, involving all five stages: "I see how threateningly confused this mess in front of me is (stage one). Nevertheless, I think I also perceive some latent pattern of order here and there (stage two). Let me start with this and then continue to rearrange it a bit more in my mind's eye; then I can work out how it would appear if only I changed so-and-so (stage three). Now what do I see? Yes, it is much tidier under this new light; I really am getting on (stage four).[9] I must apply the same ideas to my other problems; I can begin to see my way through some of them already (stage five)." These are the five stages of the system beta cycle carried out solely at the level of reflection within the mind.

Third, the process of trial and error has already been described. There are, of course, many possible degrees of guesswork or risk in any trial; sometimes the trial approaches pure insight, objective and scientific, across all five stages. In its preparation and completeness, the trial leaves only details to yield their lessons by demonstrating how they transpire in practice. Such would be the trial flight of a new aircraft, where *a priori* design would enter into every stage. At other times the trial approaches an exhibition of sheer despair, a last forlorn convulsion that might produce some result approximating to what is desired, like a man hoping to kick a stalled engine into life, or frantically manipulating the unfamiliar controls of a neighbor's television set, flickering at some critical moment. Should he succeed, he may have learned to repeat the kicking or fiddling on the next occasion. Finally, learning by instruction, as every schoolboy knows, uses any or all stages of system beta: "What do you see before we start work on it? (Can you see A?) Does it remind you of anything? (What about B?) Could you do anything with the idea that has occurred to you? (Try C). What do you think will happen? How would you know what did happen? Suppose the answer you suggest does not come off but, rather, its very opposite, what conclusions would you draw?"

The inclusion of trial and error with the three other general methods of learning as a variant of a system cycle of five identifiable stages, is not to suggest that trial and error is adequate to explain unaided all fresh and stable achievement, whether managerial or other. The calculations and designs of the second stage of the system-beta cycle among policy forming managers are not merely random responses, like those of caged and hungry rats; the creative conjecture of the manager involves the conscious feed-forward of some identifiable design, incorporating difficult and nonquantifiable concepts like systems of human values and estimates of emotional risk. The sole parallel between the learning model here described and that of Pavlovian stimulus-response is in the notion of feedback: irrespective of the amount of conscious design invested in their preparation, managers are likely to keep to courses of action that promise beforehand to produce results of the kind they wish, and to reject those courses that seem destined from the start to invite failure.

To suggest that the rat and the manager alike will tend to repeat the behavior that gives satisfaction, and to avoid the behavior seen to lead to trouble, is very different from declaring that such courses of action are initiated in each by the same (stage two) processes. Brahms, it is recorded, put aside the manuscripts of twenty string quartets before he produced the pair of Opus 51; no doubt boards of directors have been known to reject twenty well-thought-out strategic plans before putting their energies behind a twenty-first, and for every new aircraft model that flies twenty tentative designs are rejected. Because twenty did not reach the approved standard, it may be said by the Pavlovians that the twenty-first was merely another random trial, seen to be satisfactory only after it had been tested. But others might suggest that Brahms, the aeronautical engineers, and the managers knowingly design *in advance* what they are trying to do or to say, observing definable canons or acceptable rules. After they have seen what they have created, they compare their view by feedback of it with their standards, that is, with their original intentions. If the comparison is favorable, they may build further on what they have done; they may even raise their opening standards of acceptability.

If they do not like the comparison, they may abandon their half-completed work and start once more from scratch. They will, in other words, learn from their own performances, both past and recent; insofar as they are ready to reject their tentative designs for the next achievement if they, too, fall short of standard, composer, engineer, and strategist alike may also be said to learn from their future performances. This does not mean to say that, throughout the labors of composition, computation, or policy formation, there is not frequent recourse to other general models: mimesis, insight, trial and error, and even instruction. What is inadequate is the suggestion that creative development can be compared to the random behavior of rats in mazes.

CREATIVITY AND LEARNING

The act of creativity or design, as the second stage of system beta, is thus related to the act of learning, although (by mimesis) it is possible to learn without being original or creative. It is also possible to create or design the most elaborate schemes from which there can be no learning, because their outcomes are never known in practice, and so no operational feedback is possible. Examples include the election plans of defeated political parties, although the defeat itself might be a lesson to design different plans in good time for next polling day.

In general, little is known about the nature of creativity. Some fellows in the Inter-University Program said that the system beta model as a whole was useful in helping to structure the creative act (or tentative policy) as its second phase. For the survey stage (the first of system beta) required that the total setting of the problem calling for a policy be adequately reviewed in terms of system alpha, namely, of what the manager wants to do, of what is his opportunity for doing it, and of what means are at hand for grasping this chance. A rigorous analysis of all three by a group of people initially disposed to disagree among themselves on any of the elements of system alpha may help to remove the blockages to new visions of what is possible.[10] For example, the value systems of the decision makers may conflict; some may wish for strategies that maximize market share, others current annual profit, others net worth calculated by an indefinitely prolonged discounted cash flow. Again, there may be among the managers more than one questionable estimate or restrictive assumption about the external system or market opportunity, based on the shaky recollections of past success. Not a few managers struggle through their problems under a heavy burden of inherited misperception. However, a good survey, or first stage of system beta, by critically recapitulating the facts and redefining the values, especially when carried out by a group of persons with differing experiences, may free the way for new and perhaps creative ideas.

The first stage does not exhaust the usefulness of the system beta model for creative reflection or innovative design. The third stage, of action, of envisioning how the new design would need to work, may also help some strategists with suggestions for the second, particularly those managers with an operational outlook (see also p. 76). By imagining the detailed operations of particular existent systems or by forecasting the detailed operations of particular projected systems, some persons are inspired with new fundamental ideas, not merely with suggestions about minor operational improvements. Necessity is in fact the mother of invention—but only after she has been identified. For example, the daily problems of collecting the several premiums on different kinds of insurance from the same customer may determine a company to offer the whole market one comprehensive policy, covering all manner of risk and contingency: the slide valve of the steam engine that transformed the world was the answer of the boy who had become the slave of the earlier machine.

The situational inquiries listed as necessary to system alpha (see p. 73) will suggest other illustrations. In the same way, fresh ideas about design at stage two may flow from a consideration of the audit, or fourth stage, of system beta; since this stage emphasises the criteria by which the success of the action is to be judged, any reference to it will focus attention upon the basic nature of the problem being attacked or the policy being sought. An odd example is offered us by the Maginot Line: the German General Staff set out to estimate how many soldiers they might lose in attacking it, and thus whether their estimate of tactical success would be worth their estimate of human sacrifice. While prospecting the audit stage in this way, it occurred to them that there was no need to attack the line at all; it was possible to get to Paris with a simpler and less expensive design altogether, namely, to go through undefended Belgium. In general, quantitative attempts to compare estimates of the costs with those of the benefits of existing methods will stimulate the specifically situational quest for improvements: the auditor is also father to the inventor. In conclusion, therefore, whereas creativity is undoubtedly tricky, it may, if properly drilled, be more obedient to the will of managerial humanity than is generally supposed. Any imaginative analysis of precisely what is the need for innovation is bound to be helpful both in suggest-

ing where to find it and in learning from reviewing the suggestions; system beta provides a structured setting for the search.

RELATION OF LEARNING. MODEL TO PRACTICE

The five-stage cycle (system beta) also suggests a series of
reasons why managers may have difficulty in learning from their
experience. The stages will be discussed in turn.

1. *Review or Survey of Present Situation*

There may be an inadequate system for supplying the decision maker with the data necessary for his task; the need for
a system as such (and not seldom even for the simplest facts
themselves) may never have been sufficiently appreciated, even
although, from time to time, the crises of the board room or
of the manager's office have revealed the slenderness of the
information at present available about particular subjects.
Nor is it unknown for information to be available but to be
deliberately withheld, either because the subordinate with-
holding it fears some evaluation of his own performance that
his superior might use it for, or even because the subordinate
has private reasons for threatening his superior.[11]

2. *New Idea or Possibility*

Even if a reasonable system for collecting data exists, the
management may have no adequate means for processing the
information so made available, not so much for reaching
purely quantitative, technical, or organizational conclusions (such
as using a computer to determine optimum production mixes),
as for the primary definitions of corporate strategy. For
example, an information processing system may be quite adequate for keeping the workshops uniformly loaded with orders
known to have been received, but unequal to the unseen need
of the enterprise to change its product lines throughout. Sound
legal, economic, technological, and other specialist advice is
always useful to policy makers, but European industry as a
whole, compared with American, lacks the integrating function

of the corporate strategist[12] to advise its directors on the potential—and hence the development—of their enterprises as organic systems.

3. *Practical Test of New Ideas*

After a reconnaissance as to where the enterprise might be, and of what strategy it might pursue, there follows the task of taking effective action, and it is in achieving this that management at any level, whether in America or Europe, naturally faces its most severe challenge. Action to follow up any new decision demands change, and, in particular, change in the relations among individuals. Whether these individuals enjoy together the deep anesthesia of success in yesterday's business, or whether they eye each other across some uneasy armistice tolerable as the only alternative to internecine destruction, the prospect of change is likely to be abhorrent unless it is felt by those whom it ensnares as not unduly threatening to their present social or personal equilibrium.

In general, the communication systems of European industry do not bring to decision makers any clear perception of what these equilibria, at the operational levels, may be. What appears, therefore, as the most obvious and desirable decision taken at the board table may open a volcano beneath the factory.[13] It is for this reason that in the Inter-University Program the majority of fellows recommended—and the majority of enterprises accepted—the setting-up of task forces, or users' committees, to work through once more the paths pioneered by the fellows in their diagnostic phases. The aim of these integrative efforts is largely educational, to secure commitment, not to new technical or economic procedures, but to the prospect of new social relationships and responsibilities. Without these preparations, attempted change is likely to be ambushed by every unforeseen and exasperating difficulty, since success across the whole enterprise depends, more than upon any other single factor, upon the extent to which the senior management believes the need for these adjustments to be both real and important.[14] Where individual senior managers are opposed to the subordinate operational group or task force as an instrument of change, it cannot serve them as an instrument of social learning; the innovation paradox, that change demands specific action in order to be started but integrative effort in order to be absorbed, then may become acute.

4. *Assessment of Trial Action*

Even where top management can be reasonably satisfied that it has secured adequate commitment to a sound plan, it is not unknown for there to be no feedback to the decision makers — except for hearsay. Control departments, set up to monitor specific aspects of performance, such as cost, quality, delivery date, safety, unfinished inventory, machine utilization, and so forth, although they often exist, are as likely to be seen by line management as opponents out to assemble information to discredit them as they are likely to be seen as colleagues working in the same cause; this again is a state of affairs that top management can do much to correct. An overconfident manager may take the fact of getting something done as sufficient in itself, and give no attention to evaluating it once under way; in these conditions there can be little learning.

5. *Consolidation of Experience*

In the final analysis, whether or not management is able permanently to learn from its new experience depends upon how far it is able to see this experience as an organic unity, and in particular whether, on recapitulating its experience through the first four stages of the system cycle, it is able to project what it has learned into the future or upon other unsolved problems. Generally, top management has hardly reached what seems a satisfactory way of treating one problem (or of exploiting one new idea) before it is overtaken by the urgent need to deal with another. While their own time must always be the most precious asset of busy men, however, it may still be asked whether our modes of conceptualizing and discussing strategic problems are sufficiently concise, or whether the function of the corporate strategist is well enough understood, and thus sufficiently encouraged. It is likely that some enterprises in this program will see their working parties or users' committees as growth points for a new activity aimed at the better use of top management resources. In particular, the allocation of a new problem to a task force that has recently succeeded in solving an earlier one may be seen as the consolidation of experience; some impatient administrators, however, will not give their less successful pioneers a second chance.

RELATION BETWEEN INFORMATION FLOW AND MORALE

The last section outlines a few of the obstacles to managerial learning from experience. Because information is the working material of decision makers, it may be assumed that managers who sense difficulties in getting the information they want also feel their tasks more difficult to master and less rewarding to achieve than do those to whom the channels of communication seem clear. The argument has been experimentally tested among fifty senior managers working together in a large, modern, complex chemical plant.[15]

Following several hundred hours of free interviews at all levels of the management, a set of questionnaires lending themselves to factor analysis was drawn up; that completed by the senior men comprised 112 items extracted from a content analysis of their interviews. Of these 112 items, sixteen were discovered, by a quantitative analysis of the matrix (of 50 times 112 items), to be strongly loaded with its principal factor. These sixteen may then be seen (subjectively) as divisible into two subsets of eight, according to whether they seem to touch upon a manager's satisfaction with his general conditions of employment, R, or upon his view of the information system around him, K. The eight indicators of satisfaction and reward(R-topics) touch upon salaries; methods of performance evaluation; support of top management during conflict; fairness of treatment of middle and junior management as compared with treatment of trade unions; use of managerial talents; reward of individual effort; cooperation in strategic problem solving; and helpfulness of other managers in role definition. The eight indicators of the information system (K-topics) touch upon clarity of long-term objectives; knowledge of tasks of different directors; knowledge of how own objectives are set; belief that policy makers are not too remote from points of operation; clear view of line-staff relations; confidence that foremen are adequately informed; belief that top management command an integrated information system; and confidence that any essential information can soon be found.

The views of the fifty managers on each of these sixteen topics were numerically assessed from +2, complete confidence, to −2,

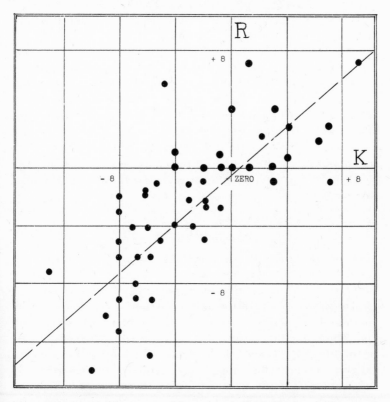

FIGURE 8(a) — Showing distribution of responses of 50 managers in same enterprise to eight statements about Information, K; and to eight statements about Satisfactions, R. The coefficient of correlation is 0.75.

total lack of confidence. It is thus possible to compute, for each of 50 managers, an average score R for the first eight items; and an average score K for the second eight items. The results of this are shown in Figure 8(a); the coefficient correlation of R on K is +.75, showing that managers who express satisfaction with their lines of communication also tend to express satisfaction with other conditions of their tasks; or that, alternatively, managers who dislike their tasks tend to complain that they get insufficient information about them. Since the factor analysis reveals no other of the 112 items of managerial opinion to be significantly loaded with this principal factor, the correlation of R and K is not likely to be explained by their common correlation with any third general parameter.

Similar results have been found in hospitals and in factories both in England and the United States. Since the primary working material of modern management is no longer coal nor cast iron but information, and since adjustment to change—or learning—is its first professional need, it is not surprising that the attitudes of managers to their work is correlated with their confidence in the system that supplies them with information about what they are supposed to be doing, how well they are doing it, where to get the resources to carry on, and other critical task elements.

SELF-DEVELOPMENT AND LEADERSHIP

In discussing the uses to which information is put during the evolution of system gamma, the need to define values is touched upon, the need to identify the scope of the external system and to assess the capacity of the internal system. In complex organizations these definitions may need much discussion with colleagues, not only to envision clearly the collective task but also to partition it between individuals, whether at the same or different levels of the management hierarchy. It is thus interesting to note that the second principal factor identified in this same study relates the self-awareness of the individual manager to his awareness of the needs of his subordinates; it may be that the interaction of these two further qualities of a leader's awareness determines the capacity of his group to adapt and to innovate, as is suggested in the earlier discussion of Figure 6.

The themes of the sixteen further items most strongly loaded with this second factor may, in turn, be divided into two sets of eight. The topics of the first set are to plan to learn from experience, to value others' view of the self, to try to recognize one's own motives, to see one's dependence on subordinates, to know persons and not only science, to value know-how as much as know-why, to admit ignorance to others, and to respect other men, whatever new technologies emerge: all of these eight may be taken as indicators of the respondent's attitude toward what kind of a person he would like to be, together suggesting a factor, S. The topics of the second set are to keep subordinates informed, to enlarge subordinates' roles, to add interest to monotonous tasks, to allow consultation to alter plans, to recognize waste of human resources, to sense lower-level coordination snags, to develop subordinates' explanatory roles, and to act only after a subordinate's report. The second eight items may be taken as indicators of an awareness of the needs of subordinates, suggesting a factor, P. The scores of the fifty managers on the eight S-items and on the eight P-items are shown in Figure 8(b) the correlation coefficient of P on S is $+.76$. This is very highly significant and suggests that self-awareness, or a recognition of one's need to learn from experience, is related to social consciousness, including a recognition of one's need to help others in their tasks of group membership. The administrator aware of his own need to profit from experience is thus likely to have satisfactory communications with his staff, and through them presumably, with the task (see p. 53).

It may be objected that the two correlations are merely at the verbal and not necessarily at the behavioral level. Two comments may be made on this objection. First, although both pairs, R and K, S and P, are highly correlated each within themselves, none of the other pairs, R and S, R and P, K and S, K and P, shows any significant correlation, even at the ten per cent level. Thus, it is unlikely that the R-K and S-P correlations are manifestations of some common bias of expression, much less of some deliberately contrived distortion of response. Second, the two relationships

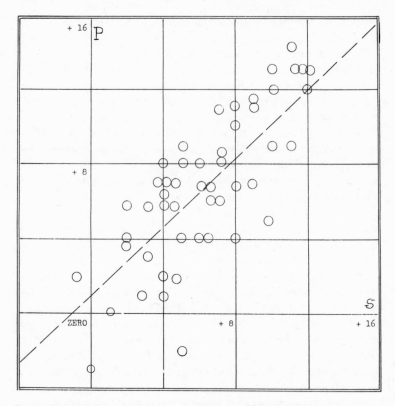

FIGURE 8(b) — Showing distribution of responses of 50 managers in same enterprise to eight statements about Self Image, S; and to eight statements about perception of others, P. The coefficient of correlation is 0.75.

may be used operationally. A series of exercises for improving R, managerial satisfaction, by improving K, managerial information, has been devised in a large factory; the exercises were made possible by first convincing the managers, from the evidence of their own responses, of the relations between S and P, namely, between self and social awareness, or between personal and institutional perceptions. Any improvement in an information system must start by observing the needs for information of the individuals within that system; these needs can be profitably studied by examining in detail the critical incidents—or operational breakdowns—in which these managers are involved.

When within an organization a sufficient sample of reportable faults is analyzed, it may be possible to suggest how operating responsibility might be more effectively distributed and, in particular, through what channels the control information might more economically pass. When this operational analysis, and the proposals based on it, are made by managers not only *within* the organization but actually *composing* it, any therapeutic action that follows is likely to be more effective than action based on the studies and proposals of outsiders, however accomplished, who do not carry emotional responsibility for the outcome of their recommendations.

In this way system beta is turned into a cycle of institutional learning. Such studies of the faults in a system set up to secure an effective division of human effort aim at an improved role-integration, under which those within the system learn to understand better, not only their own operational tasks and those of others, but also themselves and their colleagues as persons. One objective is to ensure that each has access to the information both necessary and sufficient to balance all aspects of his task, rather than more or less than sufficient for one aspect coupled with less or more than necessary for another. It is the object of much inquiry into the operational shortcomings of the factory organization to put those who must exchange critical data or information into better touch one with another. Success in these workshop exercises, judged by the subordinate managers who conduct them, seems to engender confidence in policy formation at superior levels: accepting the boss as helpful in resolving a local emergency suggests, by identification, trust in his policies in the longer term. Problem solving enables men both better to understand each other and to learn the wider objectives out of which the particular problem under review arises. Thus confidence in the policy-forming processes will, in turn, be engendered if the organization, like its individual members, is capable of learning. System gamma must become an operational paradigm. The Inter-University Program illuminates clearly the symbiotic nature of personal and institutional change: the fellows recognize the dependence of their own success in learning upon their success in teaching the staff of their host enterprises, and in being taught by them.

MANAGERIAL SELF-RECOGNITION

The previous argument, elaborating the concept of interaction between systems beta and gamma as the key to managerial learning, namely, learning by doing, may appear to exaggerate the manager's need for more understanding and a more effective use of purely external and objective ideas, and for certain operational patterns to be more vividly impressed upon his previous mental set by events occurring in the world around him. After attending a conference on productivity, for example, he might ask "Does standard costing seem good for my enterprise? What would be the problems of trying it out in the foundry, for a start? Or what about our existing distribution channels for ready-made goods bought cheaply from another maker? Could we cover our operating costs? What kind of storage problems would it give us?"

These may be important technical questions, specific, quantitative, and professional, to ask about possible new methods, but the Inter-University Program was not originally designed to spread ideas about functional specialism or other aspects of technical competence. The first objective was different: to encourage the fellow to see the management task as systemic, with himself at the center of his particular project system. However, whether an individual is setting out to learn external techniques, such as costing or market analysis, or whether he is being advised to understand himself a little better, he must still contrive to keep himself aware of the effects of his own successive actions. In this particular of feedback, the essential learning cycle remains always the same. The next interim cost statement may tell him if the new machine is likely to pay for itself or not; this will help him to confirm his judgment in technical affairs. Whether or not his new girl friend turns up for their second appointment will tell him a little about himself. If a manager wishes to confirm an emerging belief in the feasibility of standard costing in his own foundry, his best proof is to try it out in the foundry and to observe carefully the results. The manager who "proves his own work"[16] is presumably testing his own impact (such as in the consultations preliminary to standard costing), either upon some outside reality, or upon other persons; in the second test, it is not the validity or coherence of his professional skill in financial accounting that is facing the judgment of reality, but the very substance of his own and intimate self. In the Inter-University Program this second judgment was constantly expressed, both implicitly, as in the unfolding of the project that the fellow undertook, and explicitly, by the colleagues with whom he regularly monitored his personal progress.

Although many of the fellows have already written about the impact that their experience seems to have had upon them, and although an independent assessment of the program as a learning medium is also to be made,[17] it is nevertheless interesting to record here some of the impressions conveyed explicitly or implicitly, by the fellows as they became increasingly involved in the action stages of their projects.[18] They were aware that any success in persuading the management of a host enterprise to follow the advice of a visiting fellow depended much on the degree of personal identification that he had secured with the management. They soon learned that it is not alone intellectual skill nor professional competence that secures such identification.

Personality traits such as simplicity and frankness, patience and tenacity, and above all, a belief that his project was worth doing, were sensed as much to secure for the fellow the interest and attention of those in power as any arsenal of technical competence, however impressive and well marshaled. The fellows passed quickly over their early complaints about the formal syllabus: that there was no satisfactory general theory of policy formation, nor even of the administration of existing policy; that the quest for such theories is still generating a literature that, with a handful of exceptions,[19] is as voluminous as it is unreadable; that the preparatory course of two months (see p. 6) was in no degree to be devoted to instruction in "management principles," and only marginally to the techniques of operational research. It was little to be assured that they might learn better how to work with other persons and to conduct more insightful interviews; this seemed a particularly austere menu for men who, after ten years as managers, believed themselves already skilled enough in these somewhat unexciting zones of conduct. Yet the ideas hit home. As the men matured in their experiences of action and of discussing the results of action, the impressions increasingly reported by the fellows, about the teaching staff and about each other, can be found in the following analects:

> "Never tell me what you don't mean".
> "Never imply obliquely what you can't explain directly."
> "Never make yourself believe what you know is untrue."
> "Never invent the truth for other people."
> "What is an honest man, and what need I do to become one?"

The course had no prizes and no sanctions; it taught no theories and proved no principles. Nobody had any competitive reason to pass himself off as somebody he was not; each fellow was soon aware of matching himself against a practical task so far beyond his unaided capacity that he welcomed any help from any colleague at any time. This comradeship under stress nourished among them the eloquent silence of social honesty; whenever any fellow was talking of his problems before the group he became aware that the others were exchanging glances through him. In learning that others were not to be deceived, the fellows learned not to deceive themselves.

To be obliged, as the fellows constantly were, to answer the question, "And who do you think you are?" in return for the right to put it to others, is a useful exercise in self-recognition. In a climate of mutual support, it can bring to a man's notice any latent talents that, beneath his defensive disguises, had previously been unknown to him. Since there was no competition among the fellows for rewards or favors, their criticisms of each other were neither intended as gratuitous nor received as threatening. Fellows followed not only the detailed progress of each other's projects, but also the development of their colleagues as persons; they found in both project and fellow the endless excitements of a vast and unknown jig-saw puzzle, when a confident interpretation of limited data this week would be replaced by another, no less confident, the next, after a few further bits had been found and added. It was interesting to observe how these lessons, being self-imposed, were seen not as further exercises in humility but as fresh sources of personal strength. Although, no doubt, much of the mutual criticism bore a tincture of humorous malice, it was generally to the point and reserved for occasions helpful to staff and fellows as a whole.

The visit to America, bringing the fellows to travel and to live together for three weeks, and obliging all in turn to unveil their analyses and their recommendations before the keenest and best-informed critics in the world, enriched still further the learning experiences and so the friendships between these men, both staff and managers; a decade from now this group will have endowed Belgian industry with an influence for open and disinterested dealing between the enterprises in which they will by then hold commanding positions. This commerce will be system beta on a national scale. In part their friendships seem to have grown from a fuller awareness of themselves and of their latent capacities for self-expression; not seldom it was helped by the discovery that particular fellows, whose intellectual qualities others could respect, were as much at a loss in the face of reality as they themselves. In part it has grown from a heightened social confidence; the fellows have learned what it is to be supported by colleagues who ask no price for their support, and they, too, know what it is to give disinterested support to others.

Thus they now understand better the nature of true cooperation—not merely in the technical sense of holding the ladder while the other man climbs it, but also in helping the other man to be a better climber and to search more intelligently for what is there after he reaches the top. In these specific attempts to help other individuals in the program better to use their own abilities, each fellow also learned how, in some degree, to identify and himself to use the skills and talents of others—perhaps the essential quality of any top manager. But they will be plunged back among colleagues who have not been encouraged to ask themselves who they think they are, or what they think they are trying to do, or even why they say the things they do. Although each enterprise is planning to re-employ its fellow where his new experience and new self-awareness will also be an educational influence upon the organization itself; and although the presidents of the companies know that they must personally support both their returning fellows and the nascent projects started up by their departing colleagues; nevertheless, it will take all that the returning fellows have learned for them to deploy their new capacities with benefit to all. Three years from now there may well be enough results of the program for the staff to devise one much better.[20] The greatest testimonial to the present program would be to learn so much from it that it was redesigned out of all recognition, to become its own successor.

SOPHISTICATION IN LEARNING AND CREATIVITY

It has so far been assumed that managers, in addressing themselves to action, bear in mind all five stages of the system-beta cycle. This assumption may be very far from true; apart from inclination and inheritance, lack of time alone must forbid that managers have invariable recourse to rationality. But the system-beta model may, nevertheless, be invoked to estimate the maturation level of the decisions taken by any individual: his development may be measured by the extent to which the successive stages are gradually incorporated into the total response of the learner to the learning situation.

In a primitive condition the organism may respond involuntarily to an unusual input as early as at stage one; a strange signal entering the existing store of knowledge (consciousness) is likely to produce some kind of response. The Roman Senate, observing unusual movements among the jackdaws on the Capitol, would at once renew their persecution of the Christians; the traveler with the ill-omened horoscope will forthwith change to a flight number not divisible by seven. No attempts need be made, as in stage two to relate the new input to existing or stored patterns, nor to find structure, even apparent structure, common between the new and the old knowledge; the reaction may also, of course, be instinctive, as in the blinking of the eyelids when the subject is threatened by a blow, or it may be of confusion, as when a bishop might be unexpectedly corrected by a child on a point of theology during his sermon in the cathedral.

In general, however, direct response to the first input, unrelated to the rest of the system-beta cycle, is confined to primitive cultures, to children, or to nonliterate adults. At a level above instinctive withdrawal, the response, however arbitrary it may seem, is probably assimilated to animism, in which for different individuals specific inputs invoke specific responses. A poor sales return is seen (with hindsight) as obvious because the promotional campaign opened on the thirteenth day of the month; the brave spirit of the machine is seen as fighting unsuccessfully with the demon of the metal and, sinking in the exhaustion of defeat, is driven into producing spoiled work; the retailer runs out of British-style sherry on Christmas Eve, in a commercial world of pure chance and of sheer luck, where the statistical relations between demand and supply required by stage two of system beta are yet unknown, and would, if proposed at once be ridiculed. The Stock Exchange was once rich in its individual signs and systems; different speculators were guided in their sales and purchases by the movements of a wide variety of leading shares, sometimes those whose names had the same initials as their own. Guidance by tea-leaves was reserved largely for wives and for typing pools. This immediate and unreflecting response can be called "action under magic," with every different magician secure within the secrets of his own repertoire.[21]

At a slightly more mature level, the response of the subject may follow the exploration of stage two. The new input is now seen as related to other patterns held within the memory, or it produces new patterns that bear a stimulating relation to patterns already known. Beyond this, however, the response does not go, there is no accurate specification of action at stage three to be checked by the searching audit of stage four. The introduction of stage two suggests the use of imagination, the capacity to simulate or to argue by analogy. The savage who encourages his corn to grow by continuously jumping off the ground in front of its emerging shoots, and the theorist who makes of marginal analysis (a self-evident proposition in the differential calculus) a sufficient key to his understanding of the business world, are alike frozen at stage two. They equally display imagination, but they do not pause to ask whether what they have imagined bears any correspondence to reality. They remain artists, not rational action takers, expressing the imaginative patterns of their inmost thoughts, and it is hardly for others to evaluate that to which they have no access.[22]

It is evident that many decisions are taken at or directly after stage two, wherein the manager has envisioned a plausible but untested similarity between the present situation and some recollection of his past experience. Time and again superficial resemblance is accepted as adequate ground for decision. This might be described as "action under analogy"; a classical example is Aristotle's teaching that bodies fall at a speed proportional to their weight, and, even at the level of scholarship, the Greeks hardly passed beyond analogies. One may search the majority of their works in vain for references to controlled experiment; not until the thirteenth century was the notion of objective test sufficiently diffused to offer a threat to a culture of scholarship based on the authority of elaborated logic. Most Eastern, and not a little Western, philosophy is still argument under analogy. Most formal education does not go beyond it, and it is often understood in university circles that the "intellectual" treatment of a topic is completed when a convincing logical (or even verbal) analogy has been established.

The addition of stage three is the tribute of empiricism, the acceptance of the specific practice that manifestly works. When it is discovered, after the imagination has suggested that the grove of trees may be simulated by the leaping arches of the Gothic nave, that such and such architectural constructions tend to stay aloft while others tend to fall to the ground — or that, in response to the insistent necessities of military success, the critical choice lies between the long bow and the cross — then it is not the general laws of statics nor of dynamics that are put to the test of practice. Specific answers are sought for, and are sufficient to, specific questions; there is no rigorously designed test of any general hypothesis, only a pragmatic solution for a solitary need. No variation of limits, no optimization of costs, no interaction between intermediate stages are demanded, so that the total situation might become more fully understood at depth; the yes or no of final consequences is outcome enough. The audit stage is neither envisioned in advance nor demanded in conclusion. Thus action under magic and action under imagination are succeeded, in the scale of increasing sophistication, by "action under empiricism." Note the progression from the individual choice or belief of magic, through the social or collective agreement of imagination, to the objective if limited demonstration of the empirical; these reflect the three natural stages of human development: the magic fairylands of childhood, the permissive unanimity of adolescence, and the pragmatic sanction of maturity.

When the cycle is fully extended to include stage 4, and the action is designed in a rigorous and self-questioning detail against a coherent fabric of already tested laws, it then becomes possible to trace precisely *where* the results of the action diverge from those forecast. The ambition of the audit is not confined merely to noticing whether one arch will stand rather than another, nor whether the second bow will outshoot the first; it sets out to observe, under a variety of conditions, to what extent and in what particulars their respective performances may compare. The simple satisfaction of finding out whether the response is the one or the other has given way to a detailed search for their inner structure; cause and effect interactions are now invoked, to determine how far measurable changes in particular input variables produce effects upon the output. We have reached the sophisticated levels of Fisher's "Design of Experiments" when we enter fully into the spirit of stage four; we have passed from sailing vessel to hovercraft; from balloon to helicopter; from woodworker's lathe to computer-controlled profiling cutter, after we have added stage four to the previous three. It is a long step from accepting the collapse of the cathedral spire as a warning of God's displeasure. We may suggest that, when stage four is observed, we are promoting "action under design," and learning, not by magic, not by analogy, not by empiricism, but by the scientific method in all its completeness.

In this recapitulation of the system-beta cycle the significance of stage five — control, namely, the incorporation or rejection of the action pattern — is universal. The arbitrary response directly to stage one will reinforce an existing belief in magic, or in the influences of particular tutelary spirits watching over particular events. If a vivid response ensues, the spirit is in a good humor; if it does not, the spirit must be propitiated. The imaginative decision taken after reflection during stage two will be recounted to and (perhaps) approved of by others; there will be inscribed some new chapter in the folklore, the old wives' tales will be retold anew and the case study leaders will rack their brains for similar anecdotes to lend still further support. The engineer's solution stumbled upon after stage three will be demonstrated on the visit to the mine, a long paper showing *exactly* how the new airway was constructed and specifying *exactly* the horsepower of the motors, the angle of the fan blades, and many other technical details, will appear in the Proceedings of the Institution of Mining Engineers; from this it will be copied in *exact* detail, even to the point of such irrelevancies as the *exact* color of the paint on the guard rails and the *exact* gauge of any tracks that run into the workings. It is this emergence of stage 3, as the mimesis of successful empiricism, or copying without insight, that makes it possible for a British steam locomotive to end its days on American tracks. The modern gauge of 4 feet, $8\frac{1}{2}$ inches can be traced back to the eighteenth-century horse-trams of a colliery in Durham.

Finally, not only the demonstration of the particular example, but also the proof of the general law, that is implied by stage four, leads to the structured extension of theoretical ideas. The report of the scientist on his experiment is rich in references to other work, to opposing theories and, distinctively, to the outer unknowns; it will suggest not only what has been proved by his experiments, but also what is yet needed to be proved, and it is the incorporation into the literature of what has been done in the first four stages that is now truly stage five. Thus there are *a priori* reasons for suggesting that action, or creativity, can depend—and, in its evolution through both the individual and the culture, will so depend—successively upon magic, imagination, empiricism, and design. In trying to assist the creative potential of managers, a theory of learning based on the last of these has been chosen.

In practice, any given manager is normally in the course of handling many decisions over the same period. One hundred is the order of magnitude of the total problems currently engaging the manager of a medium-sized factory. Some of these may call for a long series of interlocking decisions, and any given manager may treat any of these by magic, imagination, empiricism, or design. What would seem important is that the manager's most precious asset, his time, is effectively allocated; if magic is speedy, let it be used often on the decisions that do not matter, such as the precise aroma for the canteen and kitchen aerosols; if imagination is also speedy, let it be freely used where, on the average, no particular harm is done, such as in making a rule that, on Monday, Wednesday and Friday one week and Tuesday and Thursday the next, the works radio is on the program plugging one kind of dog food, whereas on Tuesday and Thursday of the first week and Monday, Wednesday and Friday of the second, it is on the program that plugs the competitor brand. Action under empiricism and action under design are thus reserved for the decisions of operational and tactical importance. It is in their use that learning may arise. Given a little practice, a manager will soon recognize for which occasions they may be reserved.

HISTORICAL ANALOGIES

These four plus one stages of the system beta paradigm, reflected in the four stages of learning and creativity within the individual, are also written across the face of history. In the beginning is the heroic, or magic age: "There were giants in the earth in those days . . . mighty men which were of old, men of renown."[23] Events are indistinguishable from miracles and miracles are everyday events. Every untested chronicle is, at stage one, superstition in disguise. In a sense it is an age within the immemorial past; its heroes are Achilles and Arthur, Roland and Siegfried. But it is also an age perpetually with us; the press thrives on presenting sordid suburban incident as unfathomable mystery and in crowning upon the throne of a goddess the latest in adolescent entertainers.

This heroic age is succeeded by the religious; Homer yields to St. Augustine; a limitless hierarchy of individual gods falls before the omnipotent and universal God: "The One remains, the many change and pass." As the word itself suggests, religion is that which binds its followers together in the image of their god; the world had become, by the Middle Ages, one gigantic manifestation of the divine presence, in which all men professed the same brotherly creed, and in which the first duty of the guardian is to extirpate the heretic. The relationship of stage two does not lie concealed. It is the age of the orthodox, of concordance between the acceptable interpretations of reality; it is the age of endless argument, "in letters of opium written on tablets of lead," the age of the synod, convocation, and diet, at which truth is revealed, not by the impartial evidence of objective externals, but by the insinuating acrobatics of canonical opinion, the rock carved from the wind and the wind vaporizing from the rock. Like the heroic age, it still finds its echo in the contemporary press; the unanimity of belief reflected in the sales volume of a daily newspaper is essential to the myth of democracy.

Third, the ethic of the orthodox retreats, however reluctantly, before the remorseless and convincing demonstrations, however limited, of the pragmatist at stage three. The world *can* be circumnavigated; spots *can* be seen on the sun; the Donation of Constantine *can* be proved a forgery. Thus the stage is set for the entry of empiricism, for the great triumphs of the early machines, pumping water from the mine, blasting the enemy under the field gun, purifying the metal from its ore; and all alike without knowledge of what today is recognized as science. Agricola knew nothing of thermodynamics, the armorers of Gustavus Adolphus knew nothing of exothermic reactions, and

Abraham Darby knew nothing of the solid state. Successful action might have been essential but it was also in itself sufficient; the steam engine had transformed the world long before science, personified by the fourth stage of the system-beta cycle, could describe its function in the universal language of theoretical physics.

Most recently of all, under the ascendancy of the scientific method, this is a time that sees more change, in some aspects of human life, than all recorded history. The feedback of methodical research, in its testing of hypotheses at Stage four, not only rejects the false but structures the true. The scientific explosion threatening to drive mankind from the face of his planet may yet be the final demonstration of experimental proof. Thus we return to the doctrines of Ernst Haeckel; the record of the individual — child, adolescent, craftsman, and mature rationalist — and that of historical ages — heroic, religious, empirical, and scientific — converge and correspond. Phylogeny and ontogeny are alike the twin images of system beta.[24]

MANAGEMENT COMPARISONS

This brief excursion into metaphysics is tabulated in Figure 9. This relates the process of creativity, learning, and decision not only to the depth at which it involves the system-beta cycle, but also to the prevailing cultural climate, to the equivalent age of the individual, and to the characteristic epoch. All alike are relative; an industrialized society can show flashes of magic, a man of sixty may display the impulse of a child, and the romantic age may reappear when the bishop offers his benediction to the atomic missile.

It remains to add a final column, describing the correlated styles of management, all of which have been encountered during the unfolding of the projects. To the extent that the behavior of managers reflects their capacity to learn, and to develop from that behavior, the stages are clear. There is first the charismatic, responding in his personal and arbitrary fashion, unpredictable even to his closest colleagues, impossible to follow or to replace, treating every fresh situation as one

stage of system beta	response achieved	prevailing climate	level of individual	historical epoch
survey	event observed	· magic · superstition	childhood	· heroic · charismatic
decision	relation perceived	· analogy · imagination	adolescence	· religious · romantic ·
action	trial made	· practice · rule-of-thumb	empirical maturity	expansionist mechanical
audit	results analysed	· design · structure	rational maturity	economical · scientific ·

FIGURE 9—Showing main classes of response to new event and associated climates, levels of individual development and of equivalent historical or social epochs.

The first row suggests the syndrome of immediate response to a new event; without trying to relate this to what is known or to what might follow, a response is at once made. The decision taker is a law unto himself. ("My father really was never interested in politics: you might say he was above it." Capt. Philippe de Gaulle.) The last row suggests the syndrome of responses made only after the first four stages of system beta have been explored: the climate is now one of design within a known structure, the designer is a mature adult and more opportunity to exhibit his ascendancy over the tedious routines imposed by the laws of nature upon the rest of mankind. These are the men indifferent or even hostile to every step in a rational argument, from the collection and presentation of the prime data to the interpretation of the results of having taken action; they are the grand intuitionists, the feelers of portents in the bones, the listeners to voices in the air, the leader-writers, the evangelists and those who bet upon the price of dollars. But, in a world of uncertainty and thus of risk, they must always be inevitable and they will sometimes be successful. Of these we know; the unsuccessful pass into obscurity. Yet luck does not always hold even for the luckiest; one finished his days in a Berlin bunker and another has recently been returned to a small village in France. For all that, their mystical appeal goes forth to meet a public need for mysticism, for, so long as the people of the world are less than the terrors they detect around themselves, they shall still have need of their charismatic heroes.

The second type of managers are content to read their problem in the light of some analogy, precedent, revealed principle, universal creed, or other established doctrine. They do not ask that their insight should be proved, in any objective sense, by reference to the impartial juries of external observation; it is enough, for the exercise of their arguments, that two cases look alike, that there is logical comparison enough, or textual authority enough, to give conviction to the dialectically sophisticated. In management decision itself they are the dyed-in-the-wool Cartesians, the intellectual and political seekers after compromise, whether among the powerful in coalition or in the enforcement of some convenient law; for them the skills of manipulation are enough. He who, in their view, commands the wills of others may equally command reality itself. It is sufficient for them that the vote counts, not the forces of nature, but the opinions, right or wrong, that men hold about nature. In education they are the exponents of the case method, where they search, not for correspondence with reality but for correspondence between subjective impressions about particular dimensions of reality, such as finance, labor, or the markets; since their arguments do not recognize stages three or four of our paradigm, in the sense that they appear intellectually complete without them, our disputants can never be toppled from their academic peaks. In this, therefore, they have returned to the security of the schoolmen; they are the true sons of Saint Dominic, belaboring with the barbed authority of their texts the humble sons of Saint Francis laboring for their kingdom of heaven in the vineyards of practice far below.

The third class of managers are directed, not by inspiration nor by authority, but by successful and sufficient practice. Their patron saints are Thomas Edison (I've found a better way) and Henry Ford (History is bunk), although it was the great pragmatists of eighteenth-century Britain, Richard Arkwright, Adam Smith, and James Watt, who first translated the empirical doctrines of John Locke ("An Essay on the Human Understanding") into the practices of the Industrial Revolution. Within their ranks today we hear still the echoes of successful application, in the established technologies of mining, ironfounding, shipbuilding, railway transport, pottery, and textiles, those traditional industries not only largely ignorant of science but, as their expenditure on research and development shows, equally contemptuous of it. It is among these men, whose creative processes cease at the third stage of our system beta, that we may observe the most subtle antagonism to change: here are the dominant minorities, still deploying, in an unrecognized today, the policies that earned them power in their unforgettable yesterdays; here are the loyalist garrisons of reaction; here is the incense burning before the shrines of yesterday's achievement. But here are also the Goliaths who fall before the Davids and the dinosaur kings that die upon the unexpected change of climate; no longer sufficient unto the day is the evil thereof. History may be bunk, but not such total bunk that it pays to neglect the future.

The fourth class of manager is he who can not only recount his successful experience of action, but who can also explain it against the background of his wider knowledge. The steam engine evolved by empirical practice, the supersonic airliner by research and by design. The engineer of The Rocket[25] carried no tool more sophisticated than a coal shovel; the pilot of the Apollo, no instrument less so than a computer. Both may well be servants to Nature, but one has the advantage of reading her mind, anticipating her moods, and soothing the violence of her temper. It is this fourth class of manager who includes within his study of the problem the effect of his own intervention upon it, to whom the fourth stage of learning by feedback brings the final and critical meaning to his endeavor. Here is the true relativist, the systems thinker who perceives himself as an essential and flexible element in the process, the Einstein of achievement, the modern Aquinas for whom each universe of action has man at its center. The concepts of value inherent in system alpha, of feedback in system beta, and of the managerial symbiosis in system gamma, are alike anthropocentric: the observer becomes critical to the action; there is no detachment any longer, for the manager changes Nature only when Nature changes the manager. It is hoped that, even if the fellows cannot be inclined to practice the fourth kind of management, at least they are aware of its relation to the other, and perhaps more familiar, three.

CONCLUSION

The theory of learning whose inner logic is that of system beta, suggests that the recognition of one's own need to learn, the search for the new knowledge, the test of that new knowledge in practical action, the critical evaluation of the results of this test, and the consolidation of the whole exercise within the memory, are all essential to complete learning—that is, in learning not only X_1, but also in learning how to learn X_2 more easily and effectively as a second consequence. Actions based upon fewer stages of the system beta paradigm may be in themselves effective, but they do not provide exercises in complete learning; such orders of accumulated experience may be called learning by magic, by analogy, and by empiricism. The system beta paradigm can also relate the present theory of learning to other known methods, such as by trial and error, by insight and by mimesis. The theory is also related to an analysis of creativity, of decision making, and of the scientific method. It follows immediately from the study of system alpha, or the general nature of achievement. The symbiosis of a person changing a situation (action) and of the person being changed by this action (learning) embraces both system alpha and system beta, and is here called system gamma.

NOTES

1. R. M. Gagne, *The Conditions of Learning* (New York: Holt, Rinehart & Winston, 1965).

2. A deepening addiction to narcotic drugs (getting hooked) is an extreme if negative example of a regenerative learning process; in more positive managerial terms, the capacity to listen to what one's subordinates are trying to say is also regenerative.

3. When I was a boy in the Isle of Wight it was the common practice to draw the blinds at midday to prevent the sunlight from falling on the coal fire, which, it was declared, would of course be put out. Even although I could demonstrate that after a fire had been sodden with the sunlight falling on it for two hours, it could still ignite a handful of dried grass with a vigorous and aromatic roar, the blinds were nevertheless ordered to be drawn, and inquiries were set in hand as to why I had been allowed to experiment in this dangerous fashion. It is true that the sunlight is so much brighter than the glow of the coals that the fire *appears* to be out. As such it was believed, in fact, to be out and the experimental test, however dramatic, was merely a baffling irrelevance. As late as the Second World War, looking glasses were believed to attract lightning, and it was the duty of the housewife to throw towels over them at the first roll of the thunder. We may smile at these incorrigible naiveties, these blatant denials of simple verification, but as our later arguments reveal, their parallels are far from unknown to the culture of higher management. Indeed, according to *The Guardian* of May 17, 1969, the University of California has recently revived the study of astrology.

4. 9:8–9.

5. 14:8, 15–18.

6. The notion of specific instruction by feedback is also to be found in Proverbs 22:6: "Train up a child in the way he should go, and when he is old he will not depart from it."

7. "Thick glass, being stronger than thin glass, breaks less easily. But hot water breaks glass. Therefore it breaks thin glass more easily than thick glass." This argument is completely logical, but also completely false.

8. See p. 67.

9. Insight may, of course, be mixed with traces of mimesis. For example, that great forward leap in human learning, the heliocentric theory of the solar system, demanded the revolutionary suggestion that the earth is freely moving in space, not suspended from nor tangibly resting upon any other solid object. The insight called for by this departure from accepted ideas upon the nature of equilibrium may have been assisted by the unforgettable sight of the sun or moon majestically suspended above the horizon of the Mediterranean.

10. See p. 87.
11. It is interesting to examine how much time was devoted by the fellows to the supply of information to top management, *after it became clear what the information might be needed for*, that is, after the top management determined what tomorrow's line of business might be.
12. See p. 94 for ideas upon the scope of this; there is a sense in which the fellows spent their year as apprentices to this function.
13. The Ford strike of March, 1969, was based on an agreement with trade union leaders soon shown to be as much out of touch with the workers as were the officers of the company.
14. In an effort made by ten London hospitals to help each other face the problems of resistance to change, the central team, providing advice upon study methods and so forth, estimated a correlation of $+0.91$ between top management commitment, on the one hand, and the success of the projects at ward and patient level, on the other.
15. These studies were not part of the Inter-University Program that is the principal theme of this book, although their methods were also used during some of the Belgian projects, and form the starting point for two of them. A fuller report is in S. K. Sikka, Ph.D. thesis 1969, University of Manchester: "The Analysis of Managerial Communications."
16. "For if a man think himself to be something, when he is nothing, he deceiveth himself. But let every man prove his own work, and then shall he have rejoicing in himself alone, and not in another." Galatians 6:3–4.
17. By Charles Mertens de Wilmars, professor of psychiatry at the University of Leuven.
18. Incidental reports made by the fellows during the program appear in Chapter 5. I hope that the fellows will produce a book of their own experiences, a kind of collective *Ballad of Reading Goal* and *Kon Tiki Expedition* in one.
19. An exception is R. A. Bauer and K. J. Jergen, *The Study of Policy Formation* (New York, Free Press, 1968).
20. A second program was offered in 1970.
21. An experimental physicist with a doctoral degree from Cambridge is perfectly capable of treating decisions outside his own thesis as exercises in magic; he may be an ardent astrologer and refuse to sleep on the 13th floor of a New York hotel.
22. The finale of Beethoven's Ninth Symphony is a work of admitted imagination, and nobody asks whether it can be *proved*; nobody even asks whether the words of Schiller's Ode are true . . . "Joy, thou spark from flame immortal, daughter of Elysium." The work is acknowledged (proved) because it evokes complex and stimulating patterns of imagination in other persons, mostly incapable of such transportations by themselves. The artist conveys his feelings by analogy, whether in words, sound, or color. His analogy evokes not proof, but agreement, not logic but identification, not knowledge but sympathy; the greater imagination awakens the less.
23. Ex. 6:4.
24. Further analysis of our results suggests that stage two represents the acceptance of personal or moral responsibility for one's decision. Scientists, at stage four, can be entirely logical but utterly irresponsible.
25. The most successful of George Stephenson's early steam locomotives.

5

Management Education Through Action Research

Toward the end of June, 1969, when the full-time projects officially came to their end and the fellows officially returned to their own enterprises, the Board of the *Fondation Industrie-Université* decided to repeat the program. Since some members of the Board are presidents of companies that sent fellows on the pioneer program, it is to be supposed that, in taking this decision to repeat the course, they were not entirely in the dark. At the same time, the Coordination Committee of the *Fondation*, representing the five university management centers that throughout their year of project work provided the fellows with academic support, decided that on the experience gained from the program, it would be able to amplify its present policies of management education, consultancy, and research. As a first move, the Committee resolved to open discussion with the fellows, in the hope that their experience and goodwill could be put at the disposal of those professors who might wish to extend their contacts, both realistic and organic, between theory and practice.

Neither of these decisions is scientific evidence that the program was successful, or even that it was any better than the

traditional courses offered by the same centers. The evaluation of management training is a notoriously difficult task,
because normally the objectives of neither those who provide
it nor of those who submit to it are defined in detail, whether
by final purpose or by current operation; it is always hard to
assess what progress one may be making toward an unspecified
goal. Although, in the Inter-University Program the objectives
were fairly well specified, at least at a verbal level, for fellows,
enterprises, and centers alike; and although the projects were
designed around the theory of learning, such as it is, set out in
the previous chapters, a great deal of guidance is still needed
before we can confidently assert either that we know what we
are doing, or that we can measure what we have done. For these
reasons, we must learn what we can from the fellows who have
been through the program; it was, after all, they who made the
greatest investment in it, by setting aside a year of their management careers to share in what could be no more than an experiment in a field notoriously allergic to self-examination.

From the first week of their introductory course the fellows
had been encouraged to discuss what progress they believed
they were making, or what impact the course was making upon
them. During the first eight weeks every Friday afternoon was
set aside for an evaluation session, during which the fellows met
first in three groups of about seven to discuss what they thought
they were getting, or not getting, from their new experience.
These group sessions were followed by a plenary meeting with
the staff of the centers and, at times, with the scientific advisers
to the *Fondation*. Because the introductory course itself paid
great attention both to T-group training and to methods of
interviewing, it is to be supposed that these evaluation sessions
were reasonably well received, and that they brought out something of what the fellows intended to say. One member of the
staff, at least, found them illuminating in his further reflections
upon what harm a professor might cause by trying to help men
he did not know to do better a set of tasks he could not understand. For the benefit of any others who, in some unaccountable
access of humility, might recognize themselves at times to be
in the same position, it therefore seems worthwhile to enrich

this report with the reflections of some of the fellows. Exhibited here are only a few memoranda prepared for purposes other than publication; when these pieces were composed, therefore, their authors were trying to express ideas far from the scientific evaluation of their year's experience.

· ·

The first paper was written by M. Jean Nokin, a metallurgist in charge of research in a nonferrous metal company, who spent his year studying the problems of marketing strategy in one of the largest steel-producing firms in Europe. His piece was prepared for presentation to the presidents of the five firms associated with the management center at the University of Liège (Institut de Sociologie). (Like all papers, it suffers in translation from French into English.)

AN APPROACH TO STRATEGIC PROBLEMS

1. *Fundamental Concepts*

A year ago a firm seemed to me a collection of services having between them certain formal relations well definable upon an organigram. Our course has led us, however, now to regard a firm as a system, that is, as better seen as a set of interacting concepts: these are

- The resources internal to the firm; its equipment, its network of communications (as distinct from its formal organization, its human potential, its channels of distribution)
- The objectives of the firm as displayed by its general policies, and in particular by its commercial policy, alike in the long, middle, and short term
- The environment of the firm, including not only its customers and competitors but also the market itself, particularly in its evolution and in its latent possibilities of innovation

The interaction between all these elements of the system, much more than any formal and traditional relations, is the dynamic which determines the operation and growth of the enterprise. The problem that was put to me a year ago I should then have considered as being the task of an expert: an expert in marketing, because it was posed as a question of conceiving, establishing, and defining the operations of a market development unit. I should then have started my mission by trying to apply one or other of the methods of sales organization to be borrowed from the literature of the subject; I might have tried to adapt any observations made during our visit to America. I should have become a specialist appealing to a vast experience and trying to find therein the type of structure most suitable for the market envisaged. In fact, I should have constructed my solution on a simple study of one only of the three elements of the system, namely, *the environment of the firm*, seeing the task only as fitting the new unit into the existing organigram; to me its functions would certainly have concerned only the commercial services.

But one cannot set aside in this way the characteristic and profound interdependence of all three major components of the firm as a system. The solution to the problem must be constructed, not only after the particular analysis of one function or of one service, but also upon the foundation, sufficiently broad and secure, to be gained by examining and assessing the enterprise as a whole. This way of looking at the firm is more, in my view, than taking a simple section of the whole. It forces us to focus attention upon the three basic elements. But, one might ask, is not this just to state the obvious? Do we not always think automatically of evaluating our new opportunities, or of redefining our policies, whenever we might study, for example, how to introduce a new structure or a new organization? Or again, do we not invariably consider all the possibilities of innovation or change that are open to us before drawing up a budget? It is by no means certain that we do, and in any case it is not likely to be done systemically.

2. *Methods*

To return to the practical problem: my receiving enterprise asked me to elaborate an operational network for collecting and analyzing market information, but this, taken within a synoptic view of the firm, is inseparable, on the one hand, from

- The means of focussing this information, particularly *about internal resources*, upon the needs and the experience of those persons who make decisions

and, on the other hand, from

- The decision system itself, embracing *the scale of values* and the objectives of the firm

We can therefore declare, not only that it is essential to analyze before acting, but also that it is also essential to stand back and make the analysis from a synoptic angle. Even this is only one of the conditions of analysis. The wide angle must not give merely a superficial picture: the analysis must also be made in depth. If it is easy to identify the visible facts, the structure, the materials, the working methods, the prices, and other variables with which the firm must work, it is not so easy to assess the opinions, feelings, common interests, and individual ambitions of those within it: it is hard to evaluate the essential human resources of the enterprise. And yet all agree that in the majority of cases these are potentially the most valuable assets that it commands. It is impossible to build whatever we are trying to build without having first made an effective inventory of our driving forces.

It was one of the main features of our program to make us pay attention to precisely these forces and, in particular, to grasp the difficulties of interpersonal communications (how do persons see themselves, understand themselves, talk about themselves?), and to learn the skills of interviewing, namely, to help people involved in a problem to express spontaneously their true opinions and feelings. This must be an evident condition for the success of any likely solution. Why? Because

- One's opinions, whether true or mistaken, condition one's behavior and this affects, in turn, the way the organization works; it is thus an important element in the analysis.

- The individual objectives that emerge enable a hierarchy of objectives for the enterprise to be drawn up; one sees, as it were, not only the different goals on which the individuals are concentrating, but also the over-all objectives less consciously pursued by the firm.
- Persons obliged to express their opinions are automatically forced to reflect upon them and to defend them in argument.
- Persons interviewed in the search for a solution are automatically involved in it, and, as a general result, are more disposed to help in applying it.

I am going into this because these are the key concepts on which my action has been formed. They justify the methods of examination that I have pursued. What were these?

- Interviews at depth with persons involved in the setting up of the marketing information system
- Analyses of eight actual cases where marketing should have been able to play a more effective role

3. *Studies and Diagnoses*

Using this approach, I identified

- The human resources of the receiving enterprise (values, characteristic traits, opinions, etc.)
- Individual objectives of samples of persons interviewed
- General resources, such as the network of communication and the available manufacturing capacity
- General objectives, such as standards of cost and quality
- Market potentials, such as expansion of sales volume, product diversification and more effective penetration of selling operations

The matrix of information constructed in this way led me to start a diagnosis of

- Possible strategies of innovation to meet the need for growth

· The types of information that the firm needs to assemble for elaborating these strategies of innovation
· The particular network of communication now existing that would permit the effective use of this information (e.g., what are the present obstructions and linkages?)
· The conditions under which an information unit linked to this network is likely to function

4. *Proposals*

This diagnosis in the round led me to identify some critical but half-hidden factors that forced me to reconsider my first action proposals to the management. I was asked to set up an information unit; it now seems to me that, although this is a necessary, it is not a sufficient move. We must also think about

· The establishment of a special committee charged with the treatment of the information produced by the unit
· The training of the top managers, in the sense of cognitive reorganization, to use the new unit
· The collective training of the middle managers whose work will be affected by the new unit

5. *Diagrammatic Representation of Approach*

The diagram on the opposite page, which summarizes the program adopted, clearly structures my systemic approach to the problem.

My analysis of a year ago would probably have finished at (1) (a specification of the new unit), but a systemic approach and the techniques of interview have led me now to (2) and (3), and I see them as essential to the proper working of (1). Often, in the classical approach, these elements remain hidden or over-shadowed, although they can be and often are the elements on which the searchlights should be directed.

Concepts emerging as outputs	strategic plan	management by objectives	knowledge of needs of firm
	interlocking objectives	economy in use of managerial time	
	policy for needs		
Proposals	establishment of committee (3)	training of directors and middle managers (2)	specification of new unit (1)
Diagnoses	improved network of communications (i)	conditions in which unit may effectively operate (j)	types of data necessary (h)
			possible plans for development (g)
Studies	human resources (f)	general goals	market potentials (c)
	individual goals (e)	general resources (d)	
Methods	interviews		eight case studies
System elements	objectives (b)	internal resources (a)	market opportunities
Primary input as concept	firm considered as an interacting system		

(a) Human potential, communication system, equipment, working capital, etc.
(b) Commerical policy in its widest aspects.
(c) Further penetration of the market, product development, market analysis, diversification.
(d) Strong and weak points, equipment, skills, distribution channels.
(e) Motivations of different services or of different individuals.
(f) Values and skills of men and of groups.
(g) To be developed and applied.
(h) To elaborate a set of procedures and rules.
(i) To apply and process the information.
(j) To influence the network of communications.

6. *Output Concepts*

As each of my proposals is put forward, a series of concepts must be explained:

External resources; antennae: Should the search of the potential market be biased toward technique, sales, or the economy? The answer, once more, depends upon the particular case. In my project, one is inclined to look for a business analyst, capable of examining the environment in terms of technical ideas thrown up by the research and development staff. This must always be the starting point for a firm traditionally centered upon its internal resources.

Objectives; management committee: An active group is needed, balanced both in disciplines and in personalities, and charged with

(a) The establishment of a strategic plan; the necessary balance is to avoid contradictions between objectives, such as

> production: to increase gross tonnage
> sales: to stabilize orders
> R and D: to innovate at any cost
> budget: to maintain a program bureaucratically prepared

If there is a proper balance among these parties the result can only be a common objective of improved return on investment, and

(b) Determining a policy for needs, that is, how to transform technical novelty into something economically productive

Internal resources; planned education: The committee must establish an educational policy

(c) To incline the directors towards the long term in the matter of management by rules and procedures (management by objectives)

(d) To give them more time to consider problems of management as such

(e) To motivate the middle management towards the problems of commercial policy

The role of this management committee is fundamental, and it is useful to extend the definition of it a little:

> Its first purpose is, as seen in this project, naturally to receive information from its antennae, but it must also use this information to guide the constructive development of the enterprise. What does this mean in practice? Its first specific goal is the strategic plan, drawn up for five, six, or seven years, based partly on internal technical ideas (PUSH) and partly on external information about market needs (PULL); the plan must be constructed upon
>
> · A product policy
> · A price and distribution policy
> · A marketing policy
> · A personnel policy
>
> · Its second specific goal is to lay down operating budgets on a yearly basis, with operations clearly stated in figures of cost and income, as well as in technical quantities, such as plant utilization in hours or product volumes in tons.
> · Its third goal is to prepare a model of the firm, showing its response to widely different conditions of operation, especially in the light of unforseeable changes in the environment.
> · Its fourth goal is to turn any strategy of innovation into a precise timetable, designating which individuals are responsible for which tasks and by what dates.
> · Its final goal is to introduce a system of dynamic controls, based on an assessment of operations, past, present, and future, over not more than two years, and calling for revision every three months.

· ·

This second commentary was made by Gilbert van Marcke de Lummen after his return from America; all fellows were asked to record their principal impressions of this visit, as much for the information of their own enterprises (who met their expenses) as for the scientific staff at the centers. This report concentrates on the presentation of the fellows' diagnoses and proposals for action, made to an American expert, either professor or business consultant. M. van Marcke is employed by a firm engaged in the distribution and hire of automobiles; he spent his project year studying the strategies necessary to innovation in the steel industry.

COMMENTS ON OUR VISIT TO AMERICA

These comments may be seen in several different lights:

1. A contribution to education
2. A concrete experience of American management theories
3. Its results of interest to our projects
4. Its results more specifically of interest to our normal work in our own firms
5. The relations between Europe and America

1. *A Contribution to Education*

The speedy transfer to another culture, if one is at all sensitive to the environment, is always a source of new experience. Travel is a means of self-expression, but it also allows one to feel physically, sensually, what is meant by a market of two hundred million persons, with one motorcar among every three of them: the movement, the airports, the aircraft, the hotels with 2000 rooms, the slums of Brooklyn and the skyscrapers of Manhattan, the publicity, the television, the worship of prestige, the ways of making oneself heard. It is difficult to evaluate the effect that all this has; perhaps it helps one to be more open to different conditions, to be less resistant to change—or, on the contrary, more aware of certain values, because even if one is sometimes struck by some interesting novelty, he may, nevertheless, hesitate to think of himself being led thereby into the way of living from which that novelty emerges.

2. *Contacts with American Management*

Our object lessons, based on first-hand experience and brought out vividly by those with whom we discussed our projects, have left me with several dominant ideas:

· The acceptance of the principle of a legitimate profit provides a common language for the enterprise and for its environment, not only for the shareholders but also for the public authorities. It also provides a measure of effectiveness and a means of selection, that carries to the top of the enterprise those managers most effective in using its resources.

· Guided by this principle, management displays a genuine ability to examine its own activities, its products, its organization, continually putting to itself, and at the highest level, such questions as "Is this firm adapted to its surroundings and to its goals?" The quest for means to respond to this and the readiness to act upon the response are alike a continuous source of change.

· There exists a clear distinction between those tasks concerned with short-term operations, having precisely stated objectives, and those functions concerned with preparations for the future, wherein precise objectives must yet be found. The man on the job is aware of the useful information that he holds and that he will supply if he is asked for it, but he concentrates, nevertheless, upon his specified tasks and does not attempt continually to influence the policies of his firm.

· The efficiency of all strategic planning, or considerations about the future, that is, of all sources of possible change, depends upon the involvement of top management.

· All research into and planning for the future takes for granted a thorough examination of present performances and an intensive search for their possible improvement. The accent upon the future is not considered as an excuse for neglecting the problems of today.

12

· One must have confidence in quantitative data and the objective identification of hard facts.

· Although decision is a synthesis of different contributions often best expressed through group discussions, the responsibility of the chief is not removed in any way thereby; he must still take the decision, and accept its consequences. These group discussions, nevertheless, allow the realistic and open expression of opinion among subordinate members, because of

- · A universal facility for public speaking
- · A submission to the general interest
- · Research into the understanding of others
- · An ability to concentrate on the point in hand
- · A general will to get on with the job

3. Results of Interest to Our Projects

Each project taken by a fellow to America displays two aspects:

1. *A collection of data, often precise and objective, reflecting specific problems incidentally brought up for solution.* Purely technical answers to these may generally be found by known methods of research. Insofar as they demand the adaptation of organizational structure, the introduction of systems of information or of policies for product mixes, or even the study of psychosociological phenomena, and so forth, we are already aware of the use of techniques in these areas. We all had the chance to give to the American experts as accurate an account as possible of the facts or data as we have seen them, in order to draw from these experts their suggestions about possible solutions. It is a tricky approach, because our specification of the problem is likely to be both false and incomplete, and a dialogue with the American experts is likely to be difficult. Such specialized dialogue, carried out before the whole group of fellows — some of whom are not at all involved in comparable technical projects — may have highly negative consequences for nonspecialists. It seems to me that our discussions with the American experts in these specific fields could be both more limited in scope and

more precise in aim, while being both more oriented to their particular project and better documented before they start.

2. *The introduction of a change-agent into the receiving enterprise.* His role is not well defined but his task, in my opinion, is to encourage the enterprise to discriminate between the symptoms of poor performance and the causes thereof. He is, in other words, to suggest at which places and in what sequence any change should be brought about, and to watch out that the enterprise finds within itself the influences essential to continuous action and control.

All the discussions that have helped to define more closely our perceptions of such problems, to criticize the methods of diagnoses that we followed, and to evaluate the proposals for action that we made, have met our expectations exactly to the extent that our American consultants succeeded in identifying themselves with the fellows or could produce examples of similar problems worked through elsewhere.

The accent put upon the need for us to see the permanent effects that we shall have upon the receiving enterprise, and to renegotiate over and over again our influence with those in power, has seemed to me the true essence of our learning processes. Some problems of interpretation have, of course, arisen because the relation between an enterprise and a Harvard professor or a consultant of the caliber of McKinsey or Arthur D. Little is very different from the relation between a fellow and his receiving enterprise in Belgium. Our influence even there, however, is still through our never-ending negotiations with the local management, which, although often frustrating, also teach us a great deal.

4. *Results of Interest to Our Own Enterprises*

This outcome should be integrated into a more general evaluation of the program. To what extent will the fellow feel more able, when he returns to his own firm, caught up once more by the activities that have engaged the management there over the past months? The real meaning of the program is, in my view, to be found in this question. Personally, I have been able, on several occasions, to integrate into my American discussions not only the facts of my own project, but equally those relative to my own enterprise and to the problems that we run into there. At the same time, other contacts made possible by the organization of the visit seem to me to be useful for my own firm.

5. *Relations Between Europe and America*

The interest with which we have been received, and which has been so marked in our welcome, is due, to a large extent, to the nature of this particular educational program. It is also helped, in my opinion, by a genuine concern for European problems among our consultants; this was particularly evident at the conferences we gave at other business schools. There seems a desire among the American faculty to understand better the European market and I feel that, in this respect, we should organize a more systematic contact with them and between ourselves.

6. *Final Observation*

The essence of our discussions with the American professors and consultants is in the relation EXPERT–project theme–FELLOW, and their success is strongly conditioned by the motivation of the expert and by any previous analysis that he had been able to make of our project. Although I feel that on this visit, the balance of advantage over all projects was largely positive, it would be possible to make it still more so by sending a delegate of the program to America in advance; his mission should be to prepare each discussion in detail, and in particular to ensure that each American consultant has enough information about his Belgian counterpart to draw all that is possible from the confrontation.

· ·

This third report consists of the notes used by M. Jean Moreau for his presentation to a colloqium of businessmen called to discuss their participation in the education activities of the *Fondation Industrie-Université*. Like the two previous reports it was not prepared for publication in this, or in any other book, and suffers here a little from both its inherent terseness and its translation from the French. M. Moreau, who during the program was nominated by his firm — the second largest producer of wall and floor coverings in the world — to take charge of their new planning unit, spent his year with M. Gilbert van Marcke de Lummen studying the conditions of innovation in a steel firm.

THE INTER-UNIVERSITY PROGRAM

1. *The Essential Nature of the Program*

Firms adapt to environmental change. Examples of change as reminders include

- Increasing speeds of travel
- Increasing sophistication of industrial — and of post-industrial — society
- Evolution of methods of management under the impact of mathematicians, notably in operational research and data processing; and of social psychologists, notably in the study of consumers and of the behavior of groups; and of research scientists and technologists, notably in the "forced" growth of knowledge.

Many problems are bound up with these changes:

1. Individual resistances — particularly those of the fellows themselves
2. Resistances of groups or coalitions, such as those in charge of the groups known as industrial and commercial enterprises, that seek economic goals
3. Interactions with those who are essentially the factors of change; namely, the university research workers (The universities are the traditional sources of learning and of scientific research.)

The *Fondation Industrie-Université* has thus set up a system, by which an attempt is made to bring visibly together the processes of change, of adaptation, and of learning. The system displays the essential structure of all human endeavor: goals–environment–resources, and these may be identified within an operational scheme.

Goals.

1. Education of managers (fellows participating in program)
2. Assessment of likelihood of change within, first, the receiving and, later, the delegating enterprises
3. Evaluation of university management centers as agents of change

Environment.

This is the whole economy. It is not enough to dwell only upon the rate of change, nor upon the vigor of competition, which, in any case, will be less and less confined to the traditional customers of a given firm.

In particular, the environment of our program is the totality of the twenty-one enterprises that have joined together in it. I think it essential to stress here the insightfulness of those directors (of our receiving enterprises) who have not feared – in the full sense of that word – to bring up for examination a number of their fundamental policies.

Resources.

1. Before all else are the twenty-one fellows, the first volunteers, of whom I am one, and who, in spite of management careers already disturbed enough, have accepted the challenge to rethink what they are doing with their lives. The psychological implications for each and every one of us are far from trivial, and we are obliged to call upon all our reserves to adapt ourselves to a program itself in the course of evolution. Here not only our knowledge is being tested, but equally our social

attitudes, our relations with other individuals and with the groups with whom we are confronted at our work.

2. A second resource of great importance is the knowledge we have gained from the research workers of Harvard and of M.I.T., and from the world experience of great enterprises, such as AT&T, GEC, ESSO, and IBM and the consulting firms of Arthur D. Little and McKinsey; much of this knowledge and experience we saw at the very point of its own evolution.

3. A third resource has been the discussions, the advice, and the suggestions about new approaches and new methods that have been provided by the scientific staffs of our own universities here in Belgium.

2. *How the Program Has Developed*

Our methods of study are alike dynamic, evolutionary, and realistic.

Fellow.

1. Participation of fellows in the continuous elaboration of the program itself involves

- Permanent *redefinition of aims* by cybernetic evaluation
- Use of *group resources* at all stages

2. When environment has demanded a *problem solving approach*, in a receiving enterprise and at the level of strategic planning or policy formation, where the impact of change is crucial, involving major decisions, these strategic problems have been classified under three fundamental themes:

- Corporate strategy and major innovation
- Better use of skills and potentials of middle management
- Impact of operational research and of electronic data processing on management

Let it be made clear that our energies are directed at real problems: like all real problems, ours are relatively ill structured.

3. The fellow is expected not to act like an expert but to adopt *the approach of a generalist*, using the resources internal to the enterprise itself in the search for solutions to his problems. This approach is characterized by the constant definition and reformulation of the objectives of the firm, and the constant adaptation of the firm to these objectives. In this approach we are in the cybernetic system survey–design–test–audit; observation–formulation–action–control.

4. The fellow actually lives through this process of adaptation; he himself is also changed by it. His initiative, his goals, his behavior are constantly challenged by

- The men with whom he works in his receiving enterprise
- The other fellows and the members of the scientific staffs inside the program

The perception held by the fellow of his own attitudes has been improved by certain psychosocial exercises:

- Prolonged sessions of sensitivity training
- Experience with the techniques of interviewing
- The active study of group dynamics and other social processes

Enterprise.

5. The firm has equally lived through these same change experiences as the fellow. The entry of an outside observer into the affairs of the top management leads to clarifications of view, to self-questionings, and to new insights. The kind of question first posed to the fellow has, in general, led to reconsiderations of basic policies rather deeper than anticipated.

6. It was first asked of each receiving enterprise that it should set up a reception committee (*structure d'acceuil*); this was intended to secure good contacts between the fellow and the management with whom he was temporarily to be involved. In fact, in the majority of cases, informal contacts have been so good that such committees have not been necessary, although it seems to me that they could play a most important role in

helping the change processes to develop after they have been introduced by the outsider. Such a committee could, for example, be encouraged to get something done about organizational development.

7. Interaction between enterprise and university. So far this interaction does not seem to have been very close. The university has, in this program, the first-hand chance to assess the educational needs of future managers within the economic sector of society.

3. *Progress*
Diagnosis and therapy.
  1. Period of initial training, essentially by individual reading and group discussion

     · The accent on psychosociological ideas
     · Duration: two months

  2. Diagnostic phase of making contact with the receiving enterprise and its problems

     · interviews; study of observable facts, leading to the reformulation and redefinition of the original problem

Such reframing might sometimes lead to a "renegotiation" of the role of the fellow within his receiving enterprise, associating him with a different client or client group.

All this activity is essentially the learning processes of those involved: observation, reformulation of problem, fresh hypothesis submitted to the management, second reformulation, and so forth.

3. Submission of diagnoses to test; discussions with American experts. This occasionally questioned the validity of the projects as such, but more frequently raised questions about the approach of the fellow or even about his attitudes; these two sets of encounters, on the one hand, with the professors of Harvard and of MIT, and, on the other hand, with the managers of large enterprises, produced rather different impressions. The first clearly revealed and often questioned the psychosociological

approaches of the fellows to their projects; they were mainly concerned with the *attitudes* of clients and fellows towards the problems. The second were more concerned with the search for answers or *solutions*. A happy synthesis of these two approaches was found in one firm of professional consultants.

The problems we studied were far from unknown in America. However, the attack on them is greatly facilitated there by the existence of a high level of respect for information; by management education — notably in the business schools — resulting in a much sharper perception of economic values; and by a wider view of the environment. Seen from this angle, our enterprises are in general "introverted," whereas our (American) consultants were drawn from firms much more "extraverted." For myself, and particularly with respect to my own project (strategies for innovation) the impact was most realistic, if somewhat patchy. It was the following aspects of our discussions that were to me the most instructive: the method of structuring the problem, starting with the economic environment of the firm; my own attitudes towards those in the firm among whom my enquiries were made; and suggestions about encouraging the firm to adopt measures that would ensure a continuing adjustment to change. These conversations have enabled me to suggest what course the enterprise should follow, and to see clearly the practical means of following it.

The effect on my own development has been most beneficial, first by getting a clearer view of my own possible initiatives (with our American consultants playing the roles of my advisers), then by an appreciation of what can actually be done in practice, at least in America, with concepts that, however theoretically acceptable to the academic world in Europe, have here no operational parallel.

4. *Plan for action.* On our return from America, with a tincture of Harvard and MIT still upon us, some fellows found their problems no longer to be the same. The firm had changed, the fellow had changed.

The objective of the action phase. This is not to propose a solution to be projected into the firm by some outside genius. It is the discovery of solutions by those already within the firm, made possible by the clarifying role played by the fellow. In the most successful case, the fellow has understood clearly how to negotiate his "contract" with the enterprise, and so has released the forces of action inside the enterprise itself. For example, the process of decision demands.

· Information
· Power
· Criteria, such as the definition of commercial objectives and ethical values

and the fellow may help these to be more clearly understood.
The objectives of the fellow himself.
1. The first of these is evidently to acquire a workable knowledge of the generalized management process, namely

· To be aware of, and to be able to explain, his own values and to compare them with those of others
· To be aware of environmental change and particularly sensitive to information about the environment
· To be conscious of the communications around him and, in particular, of any specific blockages to them
· To encourage the development of his managerial colleagues; it is they who, by the integration of their personal goals, their ethical values, their professional knowledge, and their motivation, finally make the enterprise what it may be

2. The second objective of the fellow is, having acquired this knowledge, to be able to use it effectively in practice.
In conclusion. I should consider myself satisfied and find myself rewarded, if at the end of my project, a number of those around me have seen that the progress and development of their enterprise is readily practicable, and that a permanent dialogue between its evident economic objectives and the personal values of those who compose it is the essential mainspring of change.

. . . .

Francis Michelet was an exception to the general rule that participants in the program should pass their year in studying and treating a strategic problem within an enterprise other than their own. Michelet was from a firm well advanced in the diagnosis of its own need to improve its internal organization (although it was not as far ahead as its top management had at first believed); he therefore started his action phase almost as soon as he had finished the introductory course. He was able to persuade his top management, as a consequence, to seek the operational help and advice of the other four fellows attached to his university center (Liége) in designing the change program of his own firm. This extract is from M. Michelet's notes to his own top management after his American visit.

Notes to Top Management

"One observes how [American] general management free themselves from day-to-day business matters so as better to think about and organize for the future of their firms. There is a vigorous effort to force the responsibility for current problems downwards; it is clearly admitted that those in the field are nearer both the sources of information and the means of treatment. The task of the top management is to give them the freedom to take advantage of both.

This policy of "divisionalization" demands:

1. A precise knowledge of the goals of the firm and of the powers granted to subordinates to help in reaching them
2. A scheme of "participative decision" involving both general and divisional management in framing operational plans
3. Sufficient freedom to carry out the policies so agreed upon
4. A system of control at two levels:

    a. Auto-control, or self-evaluation on perfectly specific activities lending themselves to local quantification
    b. Control at the level of top management, based on the principle of management by exception

It is expected that such decentralization will not be limited to directors of divisions, but will be, on all suitable occasions, pushed down to the levels of factory manager and even of section supervisor. The two arguments at the heart of this policy are

1. *The need for process and product constantly to adapt to the changing environment.* The market is constantly offering new opportunities that must be spotted and exploited at once. The entire structure of the company must be organized to keep in step with the market: total marketing control!

2. *The need to ensure sufficient motivation of management, especially in developing a team spirit.* To work for the success of the firm, all managers must see it as offering chances for their own self-realization. Their job must be an unending challenge; indeed, a challenging job seems to be, in the final analysis, a greater reward for American managers than, for example, one judged purely by its status.

The actual means of achieving similar results in Europe are suggested as follows:

1. A serious attempt must be made by the board of directors to change their conception of management: they must move from the idea of day to day control towards the idea of planning the future both in the long and middle term. It is a question of continually rethinking the future options available to the enterprise, and to contrast the existing structure of the organization with what might be needed five or even ten years from now. It is from such perspectives that the board of directors must draw its inspiration, both to adapt and to change, and this inspiration it must translate into plans and programs that must be made known at all operational levels throughout the firm.

2. The day-to-day management of the enterprise should be committed to new executive organs, localized in the operational divisions, whether by regions or by products, rather than in functional departments at headquarters. Line should absorb staff, and specialists should see themselves as being

progressively integrated back into the operational hierarchies. Each expert function must hand itself over to the generalists so that, to the benefit of the whole enterprise, it becomes one joined with its peers. The education of the entire management staff thus becomes a basic need. For the execution of the work, the accent should be placed on operational groups rather than on individuals; each group should know its objectives, its budgets, the sources of help available to it, and so forth, and its objectives should be set, not only by short term production programs, but by such variables as growth and product diversification. (In America much attention is given to open communication systems with ready access for all who might need to use information in their jobs. For example, divisional telephone networks are interconnected, with double extensions that permit group discussions at a distance, and computers are often decentralized through consoles available to isolated individuals.)

Thus, at all levels, major change should be continuously brought about, not only through technique or organization, but by changes of attitudes and of behavior by all within the enterprise. It is the outside environment of the firm, that is to say, its competitors and the development of its technology, that should stamp upon its interior the patterns of innovation. But the forces of inertia and of internal resistance are hard to vanquish, especially because any change is likely to take several years to become effective. The transition period can be most dangerous. (Many of the firms that we visited in America have been working on such changes for several years, and made no attempt to conceal either their doubts or difficulties in achieving success; for example, IBM's adventures with the 360 system. However this may be, it looks as if their flexibility, acquired by mastering the challenges posed in these experiments, is the source of the extraordinary powers of market penetration and expansion which were manifest before our eyes upon this visit.)

· ·

The fifth example of the impressions gained by the fellows is drawn from the group at the University of Ghent. When, toward the end of their year, they were invited to meet the

presidents of the firms from which they were drawn and in
which they had temporarily worked, they agreed among themselves to report on different aspects of their experience.
These are, respectively, the educational aspects of the program, the development of the projects, the content and effectiveness of the projects, and the American visit. The four
pieces are, respectively, by M. Joseph Marichal, M. Ferdinand
van Assche, M. Louis Vandermeulen, and M. Jacques Decroly.

PREPARATION AND INTRODUCTORY COURSE

I. At the start of the program, we feel it desirable that all
fellows should be told by their directors what they are supposed
to be doing during the program. Ambiguity of aims may, in
some cases, reduce motivation.

II. The six months' period of personal preparation, begun
with many different previous forms of education, gave fellows
the chance to enlarge their knowledge of the literature which,
until then, was not well known. A personally chosen reading
program should be drawn up and introduced by the staff member of each center. In order to do this effectively, the staff member should attend any interviews for selecting the fellows.

III. Throughout the preparatory phase, the center should
offer seminars to introduce to the fellows such theoretical ideas
as

·Corporate planning
·Cybernetics and systems theory
·Product policy
·Measurements of profitability
·Marketing

Such seminars, for four or five fellows of very different back-
grounds, supported by one or more staff members from the
centers, would be most profitable.

IV. The orientation program, of eight weeks, full time, should
reveal three parts:

· Fundamental organization theory

· Psychological preparation; group phenomena, exercises in leadership, and interview techniques
· Preparation of actual study projects

The principal themes for discussion should include

· The enterprise as a system
· Quantitative decision methods
· Introduction of risk into rational models
· Innovation and change in the enterprise

In the orientation course, much time was given to theoretical ideas; it would be more logical to draw these ideas from practical examples. If this were done, the program would avoid the discussion of much theory that has yet to demonstrate its practical value. In the same way, any theory of change must also be seen in the light of practical examples. Such themes could, for example, be

· The social responsibility of the enterprise
· Principles of profit allocation
· Product management and quality control
· Technical and scientific evolution and their impact on the structure of the enterprise
· Financial structures, roles of boards of management, and the interchangeability of managers
· The management gap between Europe and America
· Problems of strategy formation in the enterprise

These subjects should first be introduced as discussions of papers prepared by the staff, and then presented in ex-cathedra discourse. This method of work should be followed for all kinds of articles, chapters, and other material selected to illustrate specific themes. If this were done, it would give more conviction to the psychological aspects of the program (interview techniques, T-group training, etc.) In this part of the program, more attention should be given to the problems of listening to others, so that cross-learning between the fellows is enhanced.

The differences between fellows and staff should not be so sharply drawn. In other words, staff and fellows should follow the program as equals and prepare together its future moves. In particular the meetings that were reserved for the staff alone should be abolished.

. . . .

THE DEVELOPMENT OF PROJECTS

1. *Choice of Projects*

There is no doubt that, because of the rich experience of both the enterprises and the *Fondation*, the discussions preliminary to this experimental program could have been better structured. It is cardinal that a strategic problem must be chosen, since the program is to train future directors. This implies that the fellow should not be on some task-oriented or operational mission. On the contrary, it is clear that the mission must be to attack what is a problem for the receiving enterprise, and that the mission is thus problem-oriented. Nevertheless, the strategic problem itself must not be too sharply defined, nor the place of the fellow in the enterprise too strictly delineated. He must be given the chance to meet a wide variety of persons across the field of the problem, in order to locate the problem within the realities of the enterprise, so that he may see it in its entirety. This suggests that, at the start, the fellow should be given only a theme of orientation so that no single person within the enterprise can, at that time, be regarded as the client for whom the fellow is to work, that is, no particular individual within the department most directly interested in the outcome of his efforts. Thus, at the outset, there should be no contract, present or potential, between fellow and enterprise. Any relationship with a client and any preparation of a contract should grow as the fellow gains experience from studying the problem itself. Experience suggests that the development of his insight, the definition of the problem, the identification of the client, and the preparation of the contract are the most interesting and instructive tasks of the fellow.

13

It has also become evident, during the evolution of the projects, that it is difficult at the start (that is, in the first identification of the problem) to group the projects around a theme associated in advance with a particular university center. The true nature of each project must appear later, so that in distributing the projects among the university centers, less attention should be given to possible project themes and more to the differences between fellows in their previous university education; this would enlarge and enrich the development of the projects, and enable us to judge and to evaluate different methods of education. A discussion around some strategic theme, and based on inescapable reality, between engineers and economists, can be a lively experience for both.

2. The Reception Committee

It has also become evident that intimate and informed contacts with one other person (coordinator) in the enterprise is both necessary and desirable. He must not only show the fellow the way about the organization but must also help him in his practical moves. He must understand, and support, the objectives of the program, and must be concerned, equally with the fellow, about the success of the project. As one sees from the choice of strategic problems, the selection of this coordinator as a potential client is neither necessary nor even perhaps desirable. He may, as such, even be a brake on the progress of the project, taken in its widest context across the firm; he might, moreover, lead the fellow into sharing with him too much of the operational detail, properly the task of the enterprise. For, if the project is to achieve any significant result, the higher management itself must become operationally involved, so as by their weight to press for the most far-reaching improvements. The top management itself should, in other words, take on the principal role of coordination, whatever official contact is expected between the fellow and a member of their staff.

3. The Task of the Fellow

The very fact that we have been given the colorless title of "fellow" shows that a problem may lie concealed beneath the surface of our assignments. Many of us were even introduced into our enterprises with the harmless and discreet status of "stagiare."[1] Could the fellow's role not be made more explicit from the outset? We now see him as a change-agent, actively pursuing action research. As such, he has the advantage of seeing the firm and its problems afresh, through eyes trained by his own education and experience. The temporary nature of his assignment makes him the equivalent of an outside consultant, at least in his independence of view and in his style of working. It is his task to perceive the many specific problems that flow from the central project themes, particularly as they affect differently the work of different people in the firm, and to suggest how they may be attacked within known practical experience. He must synthesize such ideas and present them in a way sufficiently clear to the managers involved to achieve effective action.

It is especially desirable that top management should be granted some insight into these proposals, and be prepared to support them, so that, by the impetus developed, the influence of the change-agent can be translated into effective action. With such backing, it should be possible for him to set up a new work group (or to employ one already existing) in order both to introduce his proposals into the enterprise, and to continue, after he has gone home, the task that he has started. The time constraint must always be strictly observed, as extension of the fellow's mission is generally out of the question.

This work group seems an essential instrument if any proposal is to be both effective and permanently institutionalized; moreover, in order to develop strategies for change in this way, the group must be acceptable to the whole enterprise. It can be helpful in this regard if the fellow is permitted—better still, encouraged—to suggest the criteria by which such a group should be selected.

The mission of each fellow is thus to be an effective catalyzer; his proposals (that may or may not be set out in his detailed reports) should influence all levels of the organizational structure of the enterprise. Moreover, it is always a negotiated, and thus an acceptable change that he must seek. Whether or not he will succeed is also influenced, in large measure, by the manner in which the fellow is welcomed into the enterprise, the freedom of expression of the senior and middle managers and, last but not least, the backing of the president and his fellow directors. Experience has shown that those welcomes and those contacts were, in general, warmer and more open than had been expected.

At the start the emphasis was put upon dividing the stay of the fellow into two parts: the diagnostic and therapeutic phases separated by the visit to the U.S.A. Although this may be all very well in theory, in practice there is, and must be, a continual interpenetration of analysis and action. As soon as the fellow begins even to mention any specific possibility of action, this must start to influence, in a manner perhaps difficult to describe, the attitudes of others in the discussion. Often incidental questions, remote from the central theme of the project, are within the experience or expertise of the fellow, and the discussion of them can exert upon members of the staff an influence favorable to him in advancing the project. Thus, the outcome of the fellow's stay must be judged in its totality, and not by any specific results of the project alone.

4. The Exchange of Information Among the Fellows

Although the fellows are bound by common professional secrecy not to disclose elsewhere the information gathered within their projects, the exchange of ideas among them nevertheless presents a delicate problem: how far can exchanges between those within the program be permitted to go? May the exchange extend across the whole theme itself, or must it be confined to discussing only the methods for dealing with the actual problem? This is still an unanswerable question, since the opinions of most participating enterprises have not yet been sufficiently defined and compared.

5. Conclusions

In a few words: it can be asserted that, from start to finish, the project must be problem-oriented, emphasizing change within the organization. Each fellow must be clearly aware that he is acting as a change-agent. Action research sums up the objectives of the program: the development of the top managers.

. . . .

THE CONTENT AND UTILITY OF PROJECT WORK

1. *Project Themes Within the Program*

Projects can be partitioned under three main topics:

1. The use of the computer:

   ·Production planning
   ·Management information systems
   ·Introducing a new computer
   ·Administrative data-processing

These projects frequently developed into negotiations, between task forces and those whose work they affected, about what particular problems were to be treated and what priorities were to be observed in doing so.

   2. Product innovation and market analysis:

   ·To get existing departments to collaborate more effectively
   ·To rethink product mixes
   ·To get acceptance of new production ideas
   ·To strengthen staff services to general management
   ·To increase flexibility of organizations in the face of change

   3. General corporate planning

   ·To develop methods of setting objectives throughout the undertaking.

2. *Influence of Fellow upon Enterprise*

The principal determinant of a useful role for the fellow is his independence of the organization around him. Because of this, one can expect an objective approach to his project. Those among his hosts are not afraid to open their mouths in front of him, and his independent comment quickens their perception of the problem. His usefulness to the enterprise increases with the hierarchical level at which he works, and it is remarkable with what insight the visitor can soon describe the underlying structure of a basic problem. This must also be a considerable argument for encouraging the mobility of industrial managers in Belgium.

3. *Educational Value of Project Work*

The concrete action situation in which the fellow finds himself both obliges and permits him to submit his conclusions to direct test. In this way, he can improve his methods of approach or management style, in contrast to the classical seminar that cannot permit him to submit his theoretical patterns of thought to any proof in action. Another general observation on the educational value of this central concept, is that the fellow occupies a realistic position in the enterprise. It is typical of those staff members who advise the management, rather than of a specific project manager or, even more emphatically, than of a line manager. The fellow learns, in these conditions, how a fundamental problem is both perceived and attacked by the top management; how it first emerges; what system can be built up for dealing with it; how objectives can be worked out in detail; how significant in the total setting apparent trivialities can be in practice; how the line management can and must be integrated into the basic policies to be formed.

Effective tactics must declare any operational measures for carrying plans into practice, the allocation of responsibility to individuals, the provision of any necessary funds, the choice of action priorities, and so forth. The specific treatment of each project also demands knowledge of a more technical nature, such as the potential of a computer, the service that the host enterprise can offer to society, the more effective methods of interview, and other techniques of social analysis.

Another valuable product is the insight gained into Belgian

industry in general by one's firsthand acquaintance with the other projects in the program. This was a valuable product of the meetings organized by the *Fondation*, and came through in more detail during our regular conferences at the university centers and also on our visit to America. It is remarkable how similar is the situation in most of the enterprises: staff services are ineffectively deployed. This is the direct consequence of a lack both of orderly objectives, and of efforts by top management to ensure that (even if objectives have once been set) they are also steadfastly pursued and achieved. The declaration of basic policies about product lines, general manufacturing programs, development of key members of staff, research priorities, and major investment bears, in practice, little relation to the needs of action. The staff have not time enough to study such decisions in depth, nor is it generally recognized how much effort is needed to prepare them as effectively as operational success demands.

. . . .

THE TRIP TO AMERICA

I. *Description of Discussions in Various Universities and Firms*

1. *Contact with M.I.T.*

·Technical topics: Profs. Scott Morton, Crowston, Galbraith
·Psychological topics: Profs. Schein, Kolb
·Organizational topics: Prof. Myers

a. *Technical topics*
    Instructive contacts in the development of information processing; particular emphasis on the dialogue between top management and the computer to determine more clearly the multiple needs for information, and to understand in practice the integration of needs and of information; nevertheless, caution in trying to develop too fast, especially in wanting to start at the

top without first exploring the different levels of operation; it is essential, for any project to succeed, that the client is concerned in his heart with the development and installation of a data system.

b. *Psychological topics*
In this field, caution against the indiscriminate use of questionnaires, particularly in not thinking through the effect that they may have upon the behavior of the organization. On the other hand, it is imperative to make a considered analysis and evaluation of their results. Balance of power is an important element to consider, especially when there is a decentralization or a concentration of authority affecting some previous equilibrium.

c. *Organizational topics*
Integrated systems of data processing demand that one must give special attention to the training and development of staff in new methods of management; for these methods to be accepted it is essential to

·Involve the users in the definition of their needs
·Bring home to all staff the concepts of the total system
·Ensure that the system is not seen merely as an instrument of coercion

If the information about particular outcomes is known first at the top and only later at the level responsible for the outcomes, the system will inevitably antagonize and inhibit those responsible; they will see themselves always on the defensive. This reaction will automatically lead to a deterioration in the quality of the information supplied by the system.

2. *Contact with Harvard*

·Technical topics: Profs. Meyer and Raiffa
·Organizational topics: Profs. Bauer and Bower

a. *Technical topics*

It seems from these conversations that the installation of a system of data processing, particularly at the level of production control, is more likely to pay for itself by its side effects rather than by its impact on the basic problem of building the information system. In fact, solving this problem reveals the dynamics of the process to be controlled, and permits, on the one hand, the forecasting of production demand, and, on the other hand, whatever commercial initiatives may be desirable in consequence of knowing the probable short term production load.

b. *Organizational aspects*

It is clear that, in this field, it is essential to define the objectives of the organization and that these are determined by the market and by the resources; thereafter, the whole organization must be concerned in their distribution. It is, morevoer, essential to replace thinking about the *cost* of a product with thinking about its profitability; an organization must be undergoing continuous change in order to adapt itself to the evolution of the market.

3. *Industry and Consultants*

On the whole our exchanges with industry in the field of information processing were rather slender. All the same, several lines emerge:

·Policies and actions must be determined by the market
·The inevitability of realism and of logic
·Sheer opportunism

Present thinking is now profit-oriented and no longer limited to costs; in general, whether the firm is large or small, it has a precise definition of its objectives, both short- and medium-term, that flow from considering a fairly precise line of action but sufficiently flexible in the light of changes in either the market or the firm's inner resources. Finally, there is an urge to automatic control, in the sense that products or ideas no longer profitable are either given up or totally rethought.

The industrial position (in America) is thus: there is a market of which we can secure—and want to secure—n per cent; let us make for this. This is the exact opposite to the position: we know how to make such-and-such; let us try to sell it.

4. *Relations Between the University and Industry*

In general, we met young people. University staff are not appointed for life and they often have many responsibilities external to their professorships.

II. *Suggestions for Future Contacts*

1. *Contact Between Fellows and Experts*

On the whole, it looks as if the fellow who actually presented his project to the expert did not himself get much information or feedback as a result. On the other hand, the fellows not involved in his project gained the impression of substantial feedback. With this in mind, and to avoid misunderstandings between fellows and experts, we should arrange that, before any presentation in front of the whole company of fellows, the appropriate pair should get together in order to clarify

·What exactly the program aims to do
·What is the fellow's status in his receiving enterprise
·What is the nature of his particular project

There was evidently a lack of understanding on these three points by most American experts.

2. *Regrouping by Themes*

It should also be possible to group several projects according to their common themes, and then to prepare a group presentation based on them; individual presentations on each project could come together. Nevertheless, it would seem to be more instructive to organize the discussions around a number of chosen themes, each one to be prepared by a group of four or five fellows working together.

3. *Comparison of European and American Conditions*

a. *Technological gap*

Such a gap certainly exists; it consists of elements set out below and is emphasized by a different mobility of ideas. Whole teams of research workers or of innovators will leave a particular enterprise, perhaps drawn away by another firm, perhaps to set up an independent group, permanently exploiting the ideas picked up in their former employment, although motivated to do so by what their new situation has to offer.

b. *Management gap*

This gap may also be seen, and attributed to a variety of reasons:

·Inflexible conditions characterize much in European management.
·There is a permanent search for the least risky lines; we tend to make such slow decisions that they no longer refer to reality or cannot still be competitive in the market.
·Europe is more concerned with cost than profit.
·European enterprises, in general, lack well-defined middle- and long-term objectives.
·We are lagging in our ideas and concepts of education for different levels of society.

c. *Commercial gap*

This gap is one of the most obvious and depends on

·The size of the internal American market of 200 million persons

·The extent of the external market, permitting American firms to come to Europe and to set up with the help of European capital (a short-term policy, under which, to use our skills, we sacrifice other things, and in which our intellectual abilities are used on inferior tasks because we dare not take risks ourselves)

On the other hand, we must contrast these conditions with those available to us in Europe, a market broken up into a mass of enclaves

·By nonuniform systems of taxation
·By nationalist and even regionalist emphasis

This seems to suggest, at the European level, a certain multinational regrouping of several firms, in order to exploit markets not confined to one country.

d. *Gaps Due to research, investment, and politics*

These hardly need comment: consider simply the growth of such organizations as ELDO and Euratom, where the policy of "fair returns" has led to an incredible dispersion of effort.

4. *Conclusion*

In spite of these criticisms of the content and quality of some contacts, we may assert that such a visit has positive value, not only to bring out for us the different approaches at the level of the firms, but equally to clear up the mythology surrounding some management practices. But the *Fondation* might well do more about

·The organization of the travel itself
·The contacts with experts
·Cultural activities while in America
·Length of stay

a. *Organization of travel*

Regarding the many and varied interests and objectives of the fellows, we may say that, apart from one or two hitches, all went well on the tour. But perhaps fellows should have their attention more firmly drawn to

·Possibilities of tourist ticket facilities
·Car rental services and international driving licenses
·Availability of credit card services of various kinds

b. *Organization of contacts*

On the whole this was reasonably well worked out, but more attention could be given to quicker and closer contacts with the universities. More detailed and earlier contacts should be made.

c. *Cultural contacts*

We had, with the help of our organizer, a number of interesting extracurricular contacts; they should be extended and developed.

d. *Length of stay*

Two weeks was long enough for contacts with the American experts; the later presentations were obviously listened to with less attentiveness than the earlier and attracted less participation. But another week *at least* should be set aside for each fellow to organize, partly with reference to his project, partly with reference to the work of his own firm, still further contacts with the American scientific and industrial communities.

. . . .

REVISION OF PROGRAM

These are eight independent but reasonably representative commentaries on the program, and it is clear that the fellows

14

who went through it are both capable of seeing in what principles it should be improved and of suggesting what operational changes, both major and minor, should be made to improve them. On all of these points, adequate action will be taken, with the help of the fellows, before the next program is designed and made known. But the basic ideas by which the program as a whole is informed seem to bear up under the criticisms of these insightful and energetic men. After their recommendations have been tried out within their host enterprises for long enough fairly to face the stresses of reality, it is hoped that the fellows will, independently of those who organized the program and as a token of their responsibility to their own top managements and to their colleagues elsewhere in European industry, prepare a fuller report on its effects as they see them.

Such effects include those of the fellows' own long-term learning, both technical and clinical; of changes in the host enterprises, especially in the influence of their top managements; of the consolidation of the fellows into a catalyzer of Belgian industry; and of the impact made by the program upon the research and teaching policies of the university management centers. If these effects can be identified and judged, to what extent need the somewhat artificial contrivance of the program — the exchange of fellows between enterprises in order to work on unstructured problems elsewhere — be maintained?

Given that any top management will permit a free hand to a reasonably senior man from its own firm to design his own project in cooperation with a small group of identically allocated colleagues from other enterprises linked to the same university center within the program, and given the willingness of the university staff to see themselves in the role, essential but secondary, of helpers to solve problems posed by others rather than in the role of intellectual acrobats somersaulting through a bill of their own selection, then, in these conditions, might it not be possible to devise across a mutually consulting set of enterprises — or even a group of factories or divisions within the same corporate enterprise — a series of mutually instructive change programs, charged with learning processes both individual and collective? Could not we move in this way toward a truer integration of theory and practice, in which the line between management and learning about management is less sharply drawn—or even altogether rubbed out? Is it of the nature of things that the maturation of modern industrial management, demanded by the accelerating rate of technical change, must conform to a system of theoretical instruction and of abstract inquiry?

One of the by-products of administration, on the very spot, at the very time, and manifest then and there as an influence among the administrators themselves, should be a better understanding of what administration may be and how it may be improved. It is not necessarily true that only those incapacitated by the very nature of their profession from engagement in practical action should automatically be the sole, or even the principal, guardians of its heritage. The managers themselves must also enrich the arts and sciences of getting things done.

Future Developments

The future of much now offered in the field of management education cannot be foretold. The epidemics of training courses that, over the past decade, have burst upon our bewildered generation, and that have been propagated by the bandwagons, often clamorous, of quick change academics into remote corners of the economy, may yet have many years to run even in their existing forms.[2] So long as industrialists get their enforced levies returned to them by sending staff to courses, so long will the indiscriminate demand for management courses endure. Perhaps the first signs of abatement are in the renewed interest shown across Europe in the evaluation of management courses as such. The recuperative powers of a capitalist economy should never be underrated.

A prudent observer will thus consider many factors before judging either the future demand for management courses or the future resources, such as they may be, available to provide them. One element in his specification, may, however, confidently be declared: effective programs must in the future exhibit a closer union of theory and practice. Already the notion of the project is going around the management schools, taking its place in a fashion parade that has included, in their turn, work study, DCF, syndicate discussions, case methods, psychodrama, PERT, OD, and, indeed, even "all there is." But simulation by project is not enough,[3] if action still remains out there. Operational responsibility, economic involvement, evaluated participation, risk-bearing decision, consequential judgment, situational anxiety, emotional stress, threatening self-dis-closure: all these inevitable accompaniments of sincere, compromising, and realistic action, based a little on evidence and a lot on guesswork, must enter and reinforce the learning processes of those who are to devote themselves to the minatory tasks of a problem-oriented profession.

Managerial behavior is essentially behavior under stress, if not actual emergency. The scholastic roles of intellectualism, abstraction, and detachment, which, in their claims to be value-free, often cover a fear of being proved wrong, masquerading as a concern for the purity of science, are unlikely for long to preserve their traditional currency. Management students, in common with others, will increasingly demand that the academic discourse demonstrate some visible and convincing influence upon reality, direct and controllable, and that they, the students, themselves are also able to reflect in practice the relevance of the theories offered them. Simulation, however symbolically ingenious, will not suffice for a generation less patient and less impressionable than its parents.

To dwell upon the symbiosis between theory and practice, between the academy and the corporation, is an instructive exercise. To the professor it poses the questions "What is my role as a management teacher?" For it is the self-image of the professor that determines the self-images of his staff, and it is these self-images that determine their role-perceptions, and thereby the nature of the management course. Traditionally, the professor is regarded as the repository of a one-dimensional knowledge, the final court of appeal in his own specialized subject, disinterested, uninvolved, value-free, nonpartisan; he is to explain its history, its structure and its literature, evaluating its obscurities, interpreting its theories, clarifying the course of its research, relating it to other fields of learning, and, although less often, tracing its relevance to the practical affairs of our multidimensional life. His natural habitat is the study and the rostrum, and the media of his true accomplishment are the book and the word.

However, many of those who now present themselves at management courses do not want to be informed, instructed, or enlightened in particular matters of one-track book learning; they want help in dealing with the operational problems of their value-loaded managerial hyperspace—to arrest a strike, to make a profit, to meet a deadline, to decide a policy, to perfect a design. These evoke difficulties often intimate and personal, and those who seek help may need to feel intimate and personal identification with their potential helper. The academic may claim that he cannot betray his scholarship by dabbling in its possible application to worldly affairs. But where is the line to be drawn? The child may exploit its early arithmetic lessons to defraud the newsagent for whom he delivers papers; twenty years later he may use his degree in chemistry to devise new media of mass extermination. It is nonsense to enter a claim for a science that is value-free. Values are merely additional facts of every complex situation calling for human action. When the president of a company faces the indisputable discovery, made perhaps by a self-declared value-free sociologist, skilled in survey methods, that over two-thirds of his middle managers believe that they are unable to cooperate with each other because of personal jealousies on the board of directors, or that they cannot get on with their work because of constant interruptions by panic appeals from above, or because they work within no intelligible scheme of delegation, or because too many people seem to be messing about with the same problem, or because the firm has no known long-range policies, of what use is the advice of anybody (such as a value-free sociologist) not also prepared to become clinically involved in the president's own anxieties?

The professor of sociology can press upon this distracted man a marked extract from his recent speech to some conference on human relations in Bolzano, a photostat of his memorandum to the secretary of the American Psychopathic Association about seminars for the personnel directors of transnational discount houses, and so forth; all this he may do and more. But unless that president is able to identify himself with that professor as a clinical confidant, capable of feeling as he feels, and capable of acting as he might wish to act, their exchanges are no more than a waste of time, and cannot too soon be concluded.

It is clear that the fellows, too, reacted strongly against accepting scientific advice from experts who had no emotional feeling for their projects. I have heard university professors, who, before the occasion, had never been able to raise the fare out of their own country, lecturing on discounted cash flow in the price determination of capital goods to barefooted Sudanese owning no more than part share in a ruptured camel. In no sense could there be any transfer—and certainly no reciprocity—of knowledge, trust, or comprehension. These examples may be ludicrous extremes, but they are extremes soon reached within a system of instruction created, staffed, motivated, and sustained by teachers who merely have some academic speciality to air, rather than commanded by managers with urgent operational problems to solve.

If the Inter-University Program has done nothing more, it has, as the fellows suggested, at least outlined a more realistic and mutually instructive role-relationship between the professor and manager. It remains to ask whether the quest for educational viability can be taken still further.

Proposed Test of Action Model

The descriptive model of the nineteen projects elaborated in Chapters 2 and 3 suggests a simple and realizable experiment. Given that the Inter-University Program has already aroused interest among senior management, it might be proposed that, in association with future programs, Belgian industry be invited to cooperate in a sustained effort to be known as Corporate Strategy Year. In this we should touch upon that aspect of industrial policy most neglected, in the eyes of the fellows, by the Belgian economy as a whole. What, after all, are we trying to do? It is to understand, as stated in the Preface, how ideas can help to develop industry and how industry can help to develop ideas.

Our ultimate output is the symbiosis of theory and practice; that alone can extend our command over the powers of technology released by modern science. We must do more than seek to simulate this command; scientific knowledge of how the natural order may be constructed is not enough. We have to know how to use that knowledge, and, moreover, how to use it responsibly. Until now our insight into the processes of application is little but a blend of prejudice and confusion imposing themselves as wisdom and experience. A determined effort by industry, supported by the fellows who spend a year puzzling out what kind of an enterprise each had joined, and by the university staff who worked with them, to define its goals, to evaluate its resources, and to identify its problems would not only challenge the manifest national weakness, but would also meet with a response, forthcoming and positive, from the great mass of middle management who now so often regard their work with amused indifference or, not seldom, with cynical aversion.

This pervading inanition is not confined to Belgium; throughout Europe and elsewhere, the most precious assets, the abilities of middle management and of supervision, are most ineffectively employed. It is unnecessary to parade here again the arguments set forth throughout this book — what is needed is a vigorous and memorable effort to restore to each individual manager some sense of identification with how he spends the only life that he is granted to live. One practical step toward this task is for those in charge of each and every firm first to ask themselves what, if anything, they are trying to do with their own lives.[4] The suggestion for a year dedicated to the collective study of corporate strategy would treat these personal questions within the welfare of each enterprise as a social and economic organism. It would not be difficult, given a collective will toward clinical introspection, to organize such a campaign in detail.

The fellows, as their reports disclose, are now equal to advising top management, to establishing systems of search and diagnosis, to motivating therapeutic task forces at levels deep within the enterprise, and to many other technicalities of action; they would have the confidence necessary to guide the efforts of their new colleagues into promising and productive channels. The key to the program was not theory elaborated by one thinker, but practice brought about by many; not a lofty concern for the objective canons of impersonal scholarship but a struggle to grasp the slippery value systems of ambitious and impatient men. What the twenty-one fellows have learned of the conditions for successful action may already be implicit in Aristotle or Machiavelli, but if so, the fellows have at least translated such ancient ideas into the language of modern industry.

The final reports of some fellows are as closely structured in terms of the specific causes of the problems they were assigned, and in terms of the specific sets of action and subaction that are now being taken to transform those problems, as are the great tapestries through which the craftsmen of Belgium have established her reputation for all time. To identify the contradictions of ill-defined value systems and the insufficiencies of obscure information channels, to trace the failures of managerial motivation and the mistaken pursuit of noncritical issues, and to clarify a score of other questions cardinal to success in action became, under the joint influences of an orientation towards reality and the austere catechisms of their colleagues, a cultural process that all helped to develop and from which all drew confidence and administrative power.

However, technical competence is not enough. It is neither the professional experience of the fellows nor their recently gained accomplishments that alone will determine whether or not they might begin to leaven the vast and complex inertia of industrial Europe; it is also the extent to which the presidents and other directors before whom they may appear are prepared to re-examine their own roles. Management starts at the top, and is an inwardness made manifest. We might, indeed, both summarize the work of this first program and indicate the work of years to come in the words of St. Luke (ch. 17 vv. 20/21): "And when He was demanded of the Pharisees, when the kingdom of heaven should come, He answered them and said, The kingdom

of heaven cometh not by outward show; neither shall they say,
It is here! nor, It is there! For behold, the kingdom of heaven
is within you. "

An Egyptian Experiment

It has often been said that the Inter-University Program is a
product of the highly sophisticated system of management
education, singular to Belgium, that has been developed by
Gaston Deurinck over the past fifteen years. Certainly the
comments of the majority of industrial training officers, professors of management, business consultants, and even newspaper
correspondents have been to the effect that such a scheme,
involving not only the invasion of the boardroom but also *the
invasion of the boardroom by a senior manager from another enterprise,* would not be possible within their local experience. It
may, therefore, be of interest to see recounted the establishment
of a similar consortium in Egypt.

A meeting of government representatives interested in problems of productivity was held in the headquarters building of
the Arab League in Cairo, during the last week of November,
1969. It was attended by delegates from many Middle Eastern
nations, as well as from India and Pakistan; speakers came from
Western Europe, at the initiative of the Organization for
Economic Cooperation and Development (OECD), and also
from several countries of Eastern Europe.

This is not the place to review the difficulties of the developing
nations or the failure of present economic policies to arrest the
widening gap between the rich and poor nations of the world.
But it may be useful, in the context of the approach to management education described in this book, to suggest that the
most appropriate mediums for training African managers are
the study and treatment of African problems. Experts from
distant lands can no doubt bring a relieving touch of romance
to this tedious task and talk to Sudanese cotton-growers about
the alchemy of sinking funds. But it may be more relevant to the
effective production of Sudanese cotton if attention is first
given to the underlying problems of the Sudan—in particular,

to those problems seen as critical by local managers. It is not easy to say here and now precisely what these problems may be, because of the great cultural gap between the foreign experts and the native businessmen; each class works within different frames of reference, and what appears a problem to one class may be without meaning to the other.

A principal task is, thus, to develop methods of identifying and treating management problems as these are seen by the men who need to handle them. The members of the Cairo conference were therefore interested in the suggestion of an experimental program, in which, under the general direction of the Central Training Organ of the United Arab Republic and with the educational support of the Department of Business Administration of Al Hazra University, a number of senior Egyptian managers would be exchanged in order to make a first examination of the problems facing each other's organizations.

A more precise specification for this experiment was written during a visit to Cairo with two ex-fellows of the Inter-University Program: Pierre de Smet, a nuclear engineer who had spent eight months examining the management information needs of a large public utility, and Ferdinand van Assche, a banker who had identified some of the strategic problems of an international chemical concern. Both of these men were able to discuss, alike at public gatherings and in private conversations, their own action-oriented experiences and, in particular, what they felt to have been their personal impacts upon the staffs of the enterprises they had visited. Although the cultural gap between the manager from Belgium and the manager from Egypt must always remain, it is not, it seems, so difficult to span as that between the Western professor and the Arab manager. What the two Belgian men of practice had to say struck the Egyptians as simple, realistic, and, with modifications to suit local customs, well within their own resources to repeat.

Eighteen organizations[5] were committed by their chief executives to participate in a pilot program designed primarily to identify the operational problems in such exchanges. These problems were expected to arise not only within or between the participating enterprises but also within the university, for whose staff the notion of engagement in practical action was being encountered for the first time. As had been the case in Belgium two years before, it was the Egyptian managers who set the pace and who turned up in force at the public meetings called to promote this campaign in research and development. Fortunately, the professor of business administration at Al Hazra University, by his deep commitment to his newly established subject, largely atoned for the early indifference of the academic community and by the end of the week had aroused enough interest among its members to recruit the essential support for an introductory program. His example illustrates the indispensable need, in a time of change, to have within any hesitating party at least one man who believes in the new idea, whether or not he is able to demonstrate the truth of it to others.

The eighteen presidents or other chief executives of the Egyptian organizations agreed among themselves on the following strategy:

a. Three groups, each consisting of six (or more) organizations, would be formed—one group centered on Alexandria; two, on Cairo.

b. Each organization in any given group would offer the same type of management problem as the others; the three major themes would be

   i. Motivation
   ii. Production planning, flow, and control
   iii. Integration of training into working operations

c. Fellows would be of the highest possible level, generally present heads of departments or deputies to members of the policy-making board of the organization.

d. The introductory course, preparing the fellows to enter their receiving enterprises, would last four weeks, full time, and would be devoted to the following main activities:

   i. Developing the observational qualities of the fellows

themselves, for example, in conducting personal interviews or presiding over group discussions

ii. Engendering basic ideas on the nature of systems, including systems of information and decision

iii. Examining the nature of learning processes and the problems of institutional change

iv. Developing elementary skills for diagnosing management situations

This course would be conducted by the staff of the university, helped by the Central Training Organ and the Egyptian Institute of Management.

e. Fellows would be exchanged for a period of six months, during which they would spend alternate weeks in their own and in their receiving enterprises (in coming to this decision, presidents were aware of the need to lighten the existing load of home responsibilities carried by the fellows and agreed to make themselves responsible for ensuring that their fellows were able to carry the two part-time assignments; the proposal for alternate weeks to be spent at home and elsewhere was made by the fellows themselves).

f. Presidents or other chief executives would act as leaders of any working groups set up within their own organizations on the advice of the visiting fellows (this proposal was made by the presidents to ensure their own personal development as far as this was possible in a program largely designed around the needs of others).

g. Presidents or other chief executives would, under the general guidance of the academic adviser to the program, meet regularly in their groups of six (or more) to review the progress of the individual projects, of the fellows in charge of them, and of the program as a whole

h. The fellows from the Belgian Inter-University Program would remain in contact with their Egyptian colleagues, both to visit Egypt from time to time in order to judge the progress of the projects and to receive in Belgium those Egyptian fellows (and the managers with whom they worked as visitors) eventually judged to have completed the most successful projects.

i. Every effort would be made by the presidents, the academic adviser, and the director of the Central Training Organ to involve the university staff more deeply in the program, particularly by organizing short seminars on topics relevant to the three main themes.

The introductory course began in June, 1970, and the pilot program was scheduled to be finished by the end of the year, to be followed by a review of all aspects of the experiment, and a revision of its operational design to profit from the first experience.

The Doctoral Program in Management Science

On May 25, 1970, the rectors of the universities of Belgium agreed on proposals to admit for the doctoral degree in philosophy a class of management candidates whose evidences of qualification must include not only the cognitive but also the clinical; over the three years during which he is registered for the degree, each candidate must engage in the study of some ongoing, real-time development that can be shown to have been influenced in its actual execution by the work of the candidate. The doctoral program therefore includes, at the cognitive or theoretical level, analysis of the generalized management process as a compulsory subject for all candidates, whatever the special field of their research project; this generalized process is seen as an interaction between a managing individual and a managed system and is thus to be described in terms of personal feelings no less than in terms of objective models. In the final thesis, both of these dimensions of the total process must be described with the conviction of a candidate who has lived through, and been affected by, the stresses of reality. Just as the doctor of medicine is obliged to demonstrate that he can organize his many theoretical sets of knowledge—anatomy, physiology, neurology, and so forth—around the treatment of the individual patient and can carry with this integration the risk of both error in diagnosis of visible symptoms and incompleteness of diagnosis through lack of symptoms, so the candidate in management science must demonstrate his capacity for responsible involvement in the complex uncertainties of managerial reality.

In the design of this program, the influence of the Inter-University Program has been decisive. The analyses made by the fellows have finally removed any doubts about the suitability of the behavior of businessmen as a subject of scientific observation and debate. The presence in Belgium of a score of highly qualified and action-oriented men who have had the opportunity of sharing with each other their experiences of unstructured management situations provides an inexhaustible source of advice and instruction for the doctoral candidates. Nor is this all. The research projects to be undertaken by the doctoral candidates need as the first condition for success a sympathetic and understanding managerial culture; the kinds of inquiry likely to develop arguments to a level adequate for a doctoral thesis must be neither narrow in conception nor circumscribed in approach. One mission of the Inter-University Program has been to prepare the cultural acceptance of action research, alike in the worlds of the university and industry. Other influences are, of course, at work; there is a growing recognition that university education must become more relevant to the problems of the society in which the universities exist. Perhaps one contribution of the program is to suggest some forms this relevance might take.

NOTES

1. An untranslatable word: stager; one on his way; somebody somewhere.
2. In July, 1969, *The Guardian* reported a staff member of a business school as saying to recent graduates, striplings of twenty-four, "We have taught you all there is. You know you've learnt all there is . . . " The graduates themselves were described as "embarrassed by the sheer excellence of the mental equipment they had been given." On being asked "How did God pass the eternity before He resolved to create the world?" a synod of medieval theologians answered, "Absorbed in the contemplation of His own sheer excellence." But this earlier sheer excellence, although sufficient for protracted contemplation, was not, apparently, so profound as to cause embarrassment. Elsewhere the claim of the course promoter is not for unrivalled excellence, but for unassailable priority: the *first ever* seminar on corporate planning with a completely foreign cast, the *oldest established* course in business methods, the *largest* international center in Europe, the *most recent* development to be flown over from America. Two comments

made at a management conference in October, 1969 by representatives of European schools were:

"Essentially, we discuss with our students how to solve business problems, not studies about business. Secure in the leadership of Harvard, we feel no need to be doctrinaire about our methods of instruction. As an example, we are happy to use quantitative methods of analysis, but only as a tool to work with, not as an end-all. We rely on cases just as heavily as they do at Harvard, but we do not feel that we need to depend on cases in every situation."

"In covering the whole range of management education needs, [x] is fulfilling its vocation of being the European center for international management development."

One may well ask what the writers of these brave words are ever disposed to learn from their own experience .... The publicity of European management courses is best read on a roller coaster, and preferably by flashes of lightning. It seems to differ from normal advertizing in that those who write it also believe it.

3. For a critique of academic teaching methods that pretend to simulate reality, see Kenneth D. Benne, *The Planning of Change*, Warren G. Bennis, Kenneth D. Benne and Robert Chin. Holt, Rinehart and Winston, New York, 1964, p. 631.

4. The models given in Chapter 2 are proposed for defining corporate strategies at the level of the strategists. But since the projects so far have little to say on the specific, detailed, and technical operations of the men on the shop floor, these models cannot claim to be a complete set. They need to be extended, using a military analogy, from the strategic level to those of tactics and weapons. There are three levels in any complete achievement: an overall plan to implement, the organization in space and time of that plan, the detailed technical processes finally employed. In government, there must first be a policy about, say, income tax, an organization with local offices and with annual programs to fulfill; and a technical apparatus of clerks and machinery that form the cutting edge of the total system. In hospital practice, the doctor specifies the total treatment, the ward supervisor organizes its program and the nurse administers the drugs. The relation among strategy, tactics, and weapons can be generalized to policy, organization, and means; this relation deserves careful study over a wide sample of projects. (Also see R. W. Revans, *The Theory of Practice in Management.* London, Macdonald, 1966, p. 117.)

5. This later became twenty with the addition of The National Bank of Egypt and the Ministry of Education.